The Pleasantries of Krishnamurphy

Revelations from an Irish ashram

Gabriel Rosenstock

Non-Duality Press

THE PLEASANTRIES OF KRISHNAMURPHY
First edition published December 2011 by NON-DUALITY PRESS

NON-DUALITY PRESS | PO Box 2228 | Salisbury | SP2 2GZ
United Kingdom

ISBN: 978-1-908664-06-8

www.non-dualitypress.com

Introduction

Let's have the giddy world turn'd the heeles upward
And sing a rare blacke Sanctus, on his head,
Of all things out of order.

Ben Jonson – Time Vindicated

Here we have him, the Sacred or Holy Fool, Suibhne, the "File Taistil", the Hero-Trickster, the Shaman, the Indo-European mystic – Krishnamurphy. Who else ... you ask? As with the Christianity of the "Celtic world", Orthodox Christianity, and the spiritual aesthetic of the early Christians, the great religions of the East did not concern themselves unduly with the distinctions that lay between mysticism and theology. To personally experience or share in the divine mysteries and religious dogmas were as complements to one another. They were threads in the same tapestry. It was that which was believed and which was understood. In *The Pleasantries of Krishnamurphy* we are provided with mystical traces and wisdom journeys; for those who linger on the words of this text there are signposts and markers denoting the journey towards that which is accessible and yet inaccessible, those things which are understood and yet which surpass all knowledge. As a reader, it is indeed a humorous and "pleasant" journey. Who is Krishnamurphy but the holy madman, the "crazy" contemplative, the manifestation of those older and often-forgotten spiritual adepts whose unconventional and outrageous behaviour is the opposite of what it may appear, the world turned "upside-down"? His motives are human salvation and deification and his humanity is not one that is separated and aloof from nature; it is rather ontologically united with it.

His spiritual insights have a rich lineage and have been there for centuries for those with the will to explore them. They are there in the Dharmic traditions of the Sanatana Dharma, the Tantra and the Vajrayana. They are there in the traditions that are Zen, the Hasids of Eastern Europe, the Eastern Orthodox, the Sufi, the Bonpo and the Tao. They are as old as the term "Avadhuta"[1] itself. This is the same "crazy wisdom" of the Russian *jurodstvo* and the Tibetan *mahasiddha,* the spiritual unbounded and luminous spiritual "intoxication" that frequently characterised the writings of the "fools for Christ" – Saint Francis of Assisi, Saint Paul, Saint Teresa and Saint John of the Cross. Krishnamurphy is the "invisible" and universal mystic - part of his society and culture and yet not a part of it, both within and without. Krishnamurphy is "Catholic" in the truest sense of the world; he is "universal" and his universality of heart is one which is achieved through the daily practices of meditation and contemplative prayer, his undertaking of seemingly "crazy" and foolish acts, his constant efforts at transformation and divine communion. The road Krishnamurphy takes is not an easy one.

---

1. Etymology of term "Avadhuta" sourced in *Webster's Quotations, Facts and Phrases;* USA: Icon Group International (2008)

Neither was it easy for the Orthodox Saint Basil – the "fool for Christ", to name another. His travails towards sanctity or spiritual enlightenment are difficult and they demonstrate the human person in his/her absolute uniqueness. Yet he is not completely cut off from the crowd; he is a human being like the rest of us; a person whose "relatedness" to others can only really be fully understood on the spiritual or theological levels. One of the rocks on which Krishnamurphy's perspective of the "here and the beyond" holds fast is the non-dual approach – the hermeneutic perspective often referred to as non-duality.

Krishnamurphy visits the sick

'The sun has just come in the window', the old man sighs,

'Or is it I that have crept out

To greet it one last time?'

'It is both,' says Krishnamurphy, 'and both are one.'

'Ah! How it warms these old bones of mine!'

'I should turn all thoughts to the divine, should I not?

But what a pagan I've become! For me, today, the sun is God!'

'Since the sun was once created it, too, will die, my friend!

Aye! Ten million suns would not be God!' said the sage.

'But what could be brighter than the sun's rays?'

'Not your thoughts – whether they linger on the worldly or the divine.

What shines within!Uncreated! Indestructible!

Its light will shine beyond all days, beyond all space and time.'

Today the conventional "wisdom" is that non-duality should be associated solely with Eastern mysticism, Hinduism and Buddhism. But the "holy fool" who demonstrated a new way of living has been an element in the history of the western world since the very beginnings of Christianity. In the Western world the "holy fool" was he or she whose word was the "incarnation". In the same way that Jesus Christ was "the Word made flesh" and come to live "amongst us", so too with the sacred fool. Irrespective of religious formation or doctrinal affiliation, this wanderer of the interior and earthly journey was always the progressive incarnation of the Divine Unity, the non-duality that is the Divine Mystery. In the Western Christian and the Orthodox traditions, sacred foolishness was the rejection of worldly cares and the imitation of Christ who endured mockery and humiliation, the derision of the crowd. From the earliest times, spiritual "foolishness" was the challenge to hypocrisy, a challenge to pride, greed, selfishness and the thirst for power. Krishnamurphy's insights have never been as relevant as they are today. He preaches an apparently crazy freedom, the freedom from self-interest. He advocates detachment in a world that has forgotten God. He is the incarnation of the time that Anthony the Great once envisaged, that era when "… people behave like madmen and if they see anybody who does not behave like that, they will rebel against him and say "You are mad", because he is not like them."[2]

---

2. Cited in *Apophtegmy (Alphavitnoye sobranie)* [About Avva Anthony] 25 (in Russian); Vol. 25, p. 427.

Like the mystic who envisions God's eternal and perpetual workings in the soul of each and every human being, Krishnamurphy is attuned to the "spark of God", that which is always present in the emptiness. To the casual observer he might seem a "madman" or (what we in Ireland call a "chancer") but there is much more going on here:

Krishnamurphy: *Just* allow me the pleasure, the honour, to assist you in jumping out of your skin.

That is all.

If you want to jump back in again that is your own business.

Disciple: Could you put it another way?

Krishnamurphy: A thousand ways!

But what are words?

What are metaphors?

What is enlightenment?

Disciple: If you could answer that ...

Krishnamurphy: You are already enlightened – you could not be anything else – but you don't see it.

You are a candle, brimful with latent enlightenment.

I merely seek to light the candle.

What is the Word in Krishnamurphy's parables but another self-reflection of God, an intimation of the Divine Image, the pure consciousness that is perfect self-knowing and self-giving?

Jein, Says Krishnamurphy

> There's a word in German
> Not taught in schools.
> The word in question is *Jein*.
> It's a type of composite –
> *Ja* and *Nein*.
> Yes and No (Nes and yo).
> Is this a poem?
> *Jein!*
>
> Explain the Mystery of the Trinity.
> *Jein! Jein! Jein!*

The theme here is the reconciliation of the divine and the profane. But the wisdom of the Holy Fool is always taken for folly.

The Heart of the Universe

> Get to the heart of the universe, says
> Krishnamurphy,
> By hook or by crook! Or Cook.

How? ask the trembling disciples.

Understand, says Krishnamurphy,

Understand that you are not the heart of the universe

And the heart of the universe will beat loudly in you!

Through his parables and anecdotes Krishnamurphy attempts to intimate the perfect happiness which Marcus Aurelius considered the divine order of the universe; it is creation in all its fullness and intimacy, a relationship of pure love.

There is a divine order in the universe...and to discern the divine will beneath all the events of daily life and to adhere to it with one's own will was the source of all happiness. (Cited in B. Griffiths *The Golden String* (1954: p.136)

If the deepest meaning of hospitality is "receiving the Divine", then Krishnamurphy is a most generous and hospitable soul.

His is the equivalent of the Cook's response to the Disciple in *The Evolution of a Flea* as they discuss how best to search for God, how best to "realize" his hidden presence.

... when man is ensouled at birth ... the greatest longing is for the soul to awaken to its own divine intelligence, its timeless origin in divine love – limitless, undivided love that was shining forth before dinosaurs were plodding through the thickets ...

The contemplative process that defines Krishnamurphy and other "sacred fools" is not solely a journey towards transcendence; as with saints and mystics of all religious traditions it involves experiences and acts that are often painful or unpleasant. It involves the initiation of the experience that is self-knowledge and purification and the shattering of many illusions which define the much-analysed "self" as defined in the modern or post-modern epochs. Like the wise prophets of the Old Testament it involves social criticism and the stating of unpopular truths:

... What do you think of Krishnamurphy's Spiritual Anarchy?

Krishnamurphy: You don't have to answer that!

Cook: Is that what he is calling it now?

It is just having a name.

A new name.

It is not my cup of chai.

Then again, we mustn't be condemning because, as I say, it is all a matter of *syadvad*, relativity.

What Krishnamurphy means, as far as I am gathering his methods, is that spiritual anarchy is the dynamic way:

We must be bringing down the government of ego!

We must be storming the bastions
of lethargy, custom and habit.

We must know ourselves to be
awake and declare it with an
overflowing heart.

But for me, you see, the storming
of bastions is a crude metaphor:

the supreme religion is non-
violence – ahimsa parmo dharma.

This is the crux.

The core.

The heart of the matter.

The centre.

The hinge.

All is hinging on this.

Yes, the core …

The nearer we try and come to understanding transcendence and the Divine Mystery, the more difficult it becomes. To achieve a blessed simplicity or a contemplative
interiority is no easy task. More often than not, it means
to stand "apart" from the crowd, to experience mockery
and rejection in a place where there is only solitude and
emptiness, the wilderness of the Exodus and the revela-
tion of the Name, "I am". As Catholic mystic Saint Henry
Newman once put it, it means living:

> … in a way least thought of by others, the way chosen
> by our Saviour, to make headway against all the power
> and wisdom of the world. It is a difficult and rare virtue,
> to mean what we say, to love without deceit, to think

no evil, to bear no grudge, to be free from selfishness, to
be innocent and straightforward ... simple-hearted.
They take everything in good part which happens
to them, and make the best of everyone.
(From Saint Henry Newman's homily given on the
Feast of Saint Bartholomew)

The thing which the "holy fool" does the least is seek
the esteem, respect or love of others within his society.
Even his/her memory amongst the people is immaterial
or valueless. It is in contradiction that the source of his
strength and courage lies; it is in the often-sorrowful road
of the exile, he/she whose ascetic heroism challenges evil
or injustice, regardless of the consequences. Being reviled
by other people is an aspect of the sacred fool's generosity
to his fellow-man; so too spiritual enlightenment and the
gift of prophecy.

Krishnamurphy: Aurobindo says; "What men
call knowledge is the reasoned
acceptance of false appearances.
Wisdom looks behind the veil and
sees ..."

Like Jesus in his last agony, Saint Andrew of Tsaregrad
begged God to forgive those whom he had provoked to
persecute him. This is serving the world through a peculiar kind of preaching; it is often to appear "unreasonable"
and irrational in order to elucidate those truths which
others have neither the courage nor the will to make au-
thentic. Let us take an example from the Indo-European
tradition that is the (Irish) Gaelic world, one that is not
too dissimilar to many of the tragic-comic, "anarchic"

and (indeed) satirical anecdotes[3] recounted by Krishna-murphy:

An Sagart agus an Fear Siúil

Bhí fear siúil ann agus lá amháin bhí sé a siúl a'bó'r
agus bhí sé a goil thar teach pobail agus bhí sagart an
phobail agus triúr fear ag iompú cloch mhór trom in aice
an tséipéil, agus dúirt a' fear siúil leob,

"Tiubhra mé láimh chúnta dhaoibh",

Ní ra aon feisteas maith éada' air agus dúirt a' sagart
leis,

"Tiomáin leat, níl tusa le ghoil i gcúlódar fir a' bith".

"O", adeir a' fear siúil ag imeacht leis, agus bhreathna'
sé siar ar a'sagart, agus dúirt sé suas leis, "is fearr an
Té a chum ná an té a chain".

Sin é gurb é Mac Dé a chum é.

Sin é nuair a thuig a' sagart é fhéin, agus dúirt sé,

"Ó is fíor sin".

Ghlac sé buíochas leis agus cha sé ina phardún agus
dúirt sé leis gur 'úirt sé an chaint sin leis mí-cheart.

---

3. Satire as practised by the Gaelic Irish Filí Taistil (Travelling Poets) and other types of wanderers, shamans and poets can also be understood as a concept of "symbolic inversion" as common to many societies:

"Symbolic inversion" may be broadly defined as any act of expressive
behaviour which inverts, contradicts, abrogates, or in some fashion
presents an alternative to commonly held cultural codes, values, and
norms, be they linguistic, literary or artistic, religious, or social and
political. (Babcock 1978: 15).

The Priest and the Travelling Man

There was a Travelling man and one day he was walking along the road and he was passing a church and the parish priest and three men were lifting a big heavy rock near the church. The Travelling man said to them:

"I will give you a hand".

He did not have a good suit of clothes on him and the priest said to him,

"Off with you, you're not going to join any company of men."

"Oh," said the Travelling man walking on, and he looked back at the priest, and he said to him, "The One who composed is better than the one who criticised."

That was to say that it was the Son of God who composed it.

That was when the priest understood what he meant and he said,

"Oh ... that is true." The priest thanked him (for his words) and asked him for forgiveness and admitted that what he said was wrong.[4]

All religious teachers and spiritual texts request that we go back. "Go back," they say and they never stop saying it. "Go back to the Sutras, go back to the Koran, go back to the Torah, go back to the Old Testament," they say. Re-read them in the light of what we have been taught and what has already been revealed to us. In addition to their symbolic actions, the "holy fools" of the past were

---

4. *Irish Folklore Commission Archive* Iml. (Vol.) 1862: 70

courageous in their social criticism when they saw that people had taken the "wrong turn". They sought to shock them; they sought to stop them and make them think. As with the (modern) "holy fool"' Domenico in Russian film-maker (and mystic) Anton Tarkovskiy's modern masterpiece *Nostalghia* (1983), they spoke out when they had to:

> *We must go back to the point where we took the wrong turn ... we must go back to the main foundations of life ... What kind of world is it if a madman has to tell you to be ashamed of yourselves?*

We'll leave the last word to Krishnamurphy:

> ... Where do we start?

Krishnamurphy: We began our satsang this morning – as we have so often done before and as we shall in all likelihood do again – with the rhetorical question, 'Where do we start?'

We don't.

There is no beginning.

No end.

... The dynamic of the universe.

It can only be intuited – and lived – by the Heart, the Heart informed by intelligence.

And devotion.

And surrender.

Fused.

One.

Always.

Now.

Mícheál Ó hAodha,
University of Limerick,
Limerick,
Ireland

(Select) Bibliography

Boorstin, D. (1992) *The Creators*; New York: Random House

Cutsinger, J.S. (2002) *Paths to the Heart: Sufism and the Christian East*; Kentucky: Fons Vitae

Griffiths, B. (1954) *The Golden String*; London: Harvill Press

Jonson, B. *Time vindicated to himselfe, and to his honors : In the presentation at court on twelfth night.* London: s.n., (1623)

Clément, O. (1993)*The Roots of Christian Mysticism*; London: New City

du Boulay, S. (1998) *Beyond the Darkness: A Biography of Bede Griffiths*; New York: Doubleday

Lossky, V. (1976) *The Mystical Theology of the Eastern Church*; New York: Vladimir's Seminary Press

Merton, T. (2003) *New Seeds of Contemplation* (new ed.); Boston: Shambhala

Ware, Kallistos (1981) *The Orthodox Way*; London: Mowbray

The Forest Sages

Disciple:	In your wonderful discourse on the ...
Krishnamurphy:	Stop right there! No praise, please. The *Muni Suffa* says, 'Tranquil indeed the sage who steadfastly walks alone, unmoved by blame and by praise.' You were about to say?
Disciple:	Er, in your ... not so wonderful discourses on the forest sages of Thailand, you mentioned Ajahn Chan. I'm just wondering, is he a relation of Jackie Chan?
Krishnamurphy:	Best question I've heard this morning! (Except, of course, his name was Chah, not Chan ...) Anything else?
Disciple:	What about reincarnation?

Krishnamurphy:	You mean, Chah becoming Chan?
Disciple:	Reincarnation in general.
Krishnamurphy:	We try to avoid generalities here! (And generals.) That Flemish haikuist who visited us once ... writes about flies – flyku ! What's his name?
Disciple:	Is this some kind of a koan?
Krishnamurphy:	Ah yes, Geert Verbeke. Doesn't believe in reincarnation. He told me, 'Even in a previous life, I did not believe in reincarnation.'

The Past

Disciple:	I did ... bad things in the past.
Krishnamurphy:	'I' did? Who is this mysterious 'I'?
Disciple:	No, no, I, me ... I really know I did bad things in the past. Me.
Krishnamurphy:	Is the past real?
	Or just a bad dream?
	Reality is now and eternal and fully awake.
	You say 'I' and 'me'.
	Is this the same 'I' and 'me' that did bad things in the past? Wake up to the real 'I'.
	We need an I-opener here!
	What was it Yeats said:
	'I am looking for the face I had before the world was made ...'
Disciple:	But the past still haunts me.
Krishnamurphy:	Does it really?
	Does the past actually haunt you –

or are you haunting the past?
Wake up to the now and
stop annoyin' me.

Disciple: How do I awake?

Krishnamurphy: You wake up in the morning, don't
                 you?
                 Well then, every morning when
                 you awake, simply say 'I - am -
                 awake!'

Disciple: Will that work?

Krishnamurphy: What, you want me to say it for
                 you?

Disciple: How do I say it? With joy, with
                 reverence, nonchalantly?

Krishnamurphy: Any way you like as long as you
                 mean it.
                 Just keep saying it.
                 Soon you'll be saying it in your
                 sleep!

Disciple: Are you trying to convert us?

Krishnamurphy: No conversion, inversion,

perversion or anything else of the kind.

Subversion, maybe!

The lawgiver Manu suggested that conversions be outlawed.

Wisdom and compassion are enough.

A true teacher awakens these.

But you do not have to convert to anything.

The essence of all the religions is wisdom and compassion.

In fact, you do not have to have any religion at all. You can find wisdom and compassion in yourself. Have you the patience to look for them?

The desire?

If not, go home!

Disciple:	So, my sins are washed away if I awaken to wisdom and compassion? Easy as that?
Krishnamurphy:	What were your sins that trouble you so?
Disciple:	Sins with a boy ...

Krishnamurphy: Sarmad – who fell in love with a Dervish boy – says in a truly remarkable poem:

Forget the torment
the guilt of your misdeeds:

The Eye of Mercy

loves the beauty

of sin ...

Krishnamurphy and the Mullah

The Mullah Nasroodeen called on Krishnamurphy.

'I would like to have a look at your followers,' he growled.

'Line up at once!' came the order from Krishnamurphy to the sannyasins, as some of the long-term disciples liked to call themselves.

(Assassins the Mullah called them).

The Mullah whistled in astonishment, walked around, gawked at them up and down and then, gazing solemnly, in silence, a look of pity softened his weather-battered face.

'What a sorry lot!' he sighed. Turning to their Master, he bleated: 'In heaven's name, Krishnamurphy, what are you feeding them on?'

'Well, you know … they need to be sharp, so … we don't fill our bellies here, Nasroodeen! This morning, for instance, Cook put 40 empty bowls on the table …'

'Empty bowls?!'

'A lesson. To remind them all of nothingness – also of course, the Buddhist monk's simple begging bowl … the bowl of the haikuist Sant ka, gathering hailstones … and so on …'

'Rubbish! Man does not live on emptiness alone! Or hailstones for that matter! I am inviting all of them over to my place this evening for some decent nosh.'

'OK,' said Krishnamurphy, 'fine, I might get a little

peace around here.'

'Maybe I am finding some peace too,' murmured Cook who had overheard every sour syllable.

The Mullah and his donkey disappeared in a cloudlet of dust.

***

'Well?' said Krishnamurphy when the disciples returned later that evening. 'How was the grub?'

'Grubby! It was meant to be mutton,' said a disciple, 'but it wasn't.'

'Ram!' shouted another.

'Ram Ram, Gandhi's last words when he was shot,' mumbled Krishnamurphy to himself.

The disciples seemed to be rather excited or deflated to an unusual degree, the usually taciturn ones very talkative and the good communicators empty-eyed and stuck for words. Something strange has happened, thought Krishnamurphy.

'A bloody old ram!' said one, not known for his outspokenness. A chorus began:

'Yes, the Mullah's pet ram had died of advanced arthritis – '

'And sundry other ailments – '

'Tough as old boots he was in spite of the Maha Narayan oil that the Mullah applied to his joints every night ...'

'Chewing for an hour I was ...'

'Got horribly sick ...'

Krishnamurphy interrupted this sad litany.

'Dear me! Our own Cook isn't all that bad then, is he?'

Cook, lurking in the shadows, nodded solemnly, hopefully.

Krishnamurphy didn't wait for a reply. 'Did Nasroodeen not offer any sauces or condiments?'

'Ash!'

'I beg your pardon?'

'Ash!' said an ashen-faced disciple.

'*Vibhuti*, sacred ash!' said another.

'Nonsense. Nothing of the kind. Some kind of fine volcanic ash. Disgusting!' said a third.

'Totally weird, man!' exclaimed a fourth, hissing.

'Hmmm ...' murmured Krishnamurphy. 'How very strange. Did he – at least – offer some spiritual fare, some words of wisdom, perhaps?'

'Nothing. Zilch!'

'Just giggled. The man's insane!'

'Yeah, inane ... just giggled all the time, watching us eat. Didn't touch it himself, of course. And when we got up to go, all he said was, "Better than Krishnamurphy's ashram, eh?"'

The Incandescent Self

Disciple: Why is the Buddha called 'The
                    Awakened One'?

Krishnamurphy: Because he anticipated all of you
                    sleepy heads!
                    What will I do with ye at all?
                    I'm moidered. As cracked as crows
                    ye are!

Disciple: How do we awake?

Krishnamurphy: You are that already.
                    What, are you asleep?
                    Just wake up every morning and
                    say
                    'I - am - awake!'
                    Bathe in the bliss of being.

Disciple: How?

Krishnamurphy: Just allow me the pleasure, the
                    honour, to assist you in jumping
                    out of your skin.
                    That is all.

	If you want to jump back in again that is your own business.
Disciple:	Could you put it another way?
Krishnamurphy:	A thousand ways!
	But what are words?
	What are metaphors?
	What is enlightenment?
Disciple:	If you could answer that …
Krishnamurphy:	You are already enlightened – you could not be anything else – but you don't see it.
	You are a candle, brimful with latent enlightenment.
	I merely seek to light the candle.
	Nothing else.
	You do the rest.
	You are the rest.
Disciple:	How do you, so to speak, light the candle?
Krishnamurphy:	A timely glance.
	A word.
	By using every trick in the book – and a few of my own.

Disciple:	And then?
Krishnamurphy:	The candle burns. It's as simple as that.
Disciple:	To extinction?
Krishnamurphy:	Extinction of the form, yes, of the ego. What else? Allow the self to burn! This is its true eternal nature from before the beginning of time. If you go guru-hopping hither and thither the flame could easily blow out – it could disappear in your frantic seeking for that which is already inherent. There's an Irish saying, *'Ag lorg an chapaill bháin is an capall bán fút!'* Looking for the white horse and the white horse under you! Awake to the flame! Allow the candle to burn. If it goes out, it could take a long time before the wick is ready again for the flame.
Disciple:	My life's destiny is to burn? Is that it?

Krishnamurphy:	Precisely.
	Not in the flames of a medieval hell but in the fire of Reality, the light of Reality, of the Present.
	Unless you realise the fire and the light within you, you are merely a dead shape, solid wax – you are no more than a figure in a wax museum, resembling life but not truly alive.
Disciple:	You seem to be a passionate man. May I suggest that not all of us are temperamentally suited to burn, as you put it?
Krishnamurphy:	You know what you can do with temperament?
	Burn it!
	In the flame, the flame that is like a crouching lion as Yannai says.
Disciple:	Who?
Krishnamurphy:	Yannai.
	Sixth-century Hebrew poet.
Disciple:	I think you invent some of these guys. Indeed, you have invented yourself, haven't you? And so,

we came to you as you were billed
– a spiritual anarchist. Hoping
you might help us to destroy our
misconceptions. But, can you be
serious, just for a moment!?

Krishnamurphy: Why?

Burn the candle, I say; burn
the concept of the candle, the
concept of the flame until their
non-existence flares in your real,
eternal, incandescent self.

Now, let's have some poetry. How
about Robert?

Disciple: Robert who? Frost?

Krishnamurphy: *Au contraire!*
Robert Burns – who else!

Disciple: Jaysus ...

Haiku

Disciple: What is the meaning of your haiku,

fuchsia –
tears of Christ
visited by wasps

Krishnamurphy: Which bit don't you understand?

You are grasping for meaning.

The haiku that is not grasped is grasped.

That which is grasped is not grasped …

(Don't know about you, but I'm grasping for a drink!)

Riddle

It's in the water
But it doesn't get wet.
Answer?
An egg in a duck.
No, I didn't make that one up, says Krishnamurphy.
I don't do riddles:
Everything's a riddle if you ask me:
The egg, the water, the duck,
Myself. This wee poem (and the one before
And the next one).

War and Peace

Disciple: Why do we have wars?

Krishnamurphy: 'The world is enveloped in
                      ignorance,' so says the
                      Ajitamanava Puccha.

Disciple: Can we end wars?

Krishnamurphy: When the world is no longer
                      enveloped in ignorance.

Disciple: That might take some time.

Krishnamurphy: I have all the time in the world –
                      whether time, or the
                      world, exist or not.

                      We can start here, in this little
                      patch of Ireland ... ignorance once
                      fled this land in shame.

                      It can happen again.

A Fine Balancing Act

The ashram Cook rang Nasroodeen.

'How are your hens?'

'Fine!' said Nasroodeen. 'Cock is also wide awake and in excellent health.'

'Glad to hear it,' clucks the Cook. 'You can't have one without the other – though I'm a celibate myself. Can you deliver three dozen medium-size, organic, corn-fed eggs this afternoon?'

'A pleasure, as always,' said Nasroodeen. 'No bother! Can't guarantee the size, mind you. My hens have a mind of their own! Oh, by the way, you wouldn't get away with it in Rishikesh, you know! They don't approve of eggs. Take a dim view of them they do. Also, you say corn-fed eggs. You mean corn-fed hens.'

'I am just cooking eggs. I am not eating them myself!' came Cook's cockish reply.

Meanwhile, Krishnamurphy was about to take a class out on a ginko – a compositional stroll to sharpen their haiku instincts – when Nasroodeen appeared at the ashram gate. Glory be! What a holy show! He had about twenty baskets balanced precariously on the crown of his head. The disciples whispered to one another, pointing curiously at this phenomenon. One of them asked: 'Is this some kind of a Sufi ritual or something?'

Krishnamurphy blinked. 'Well if it is, I hope he doesn't start to whirl!'

Nasroodeen approached, gingerly; now and again he

would take a deep breath, steadying himself. The disciples were well and truly agog.

'God bless all here!' exclaimed Nasroodeen, wheezily.

'And God bless you too, Nasroodeen,' said Krishnamurphy in response. 'I suppose it would be too much to ask you what exactly you are up to?'

'Oh, you mean – this?' said Nasroodeen, straining to look up at his impossible load. 'Well, you know what they say, Krishnamurphy ...'

'I'm afraid I don't. What *do* they say, Mullah?'

'Don't put all your eggs in one basket.'

'Very good, Nasroodeen. You can take over today's *satsang*.'

(A talk wouldn't satisfy the disciples. It had to be *satsang*. Similarly, a private audience was out of the question. It had to be *darshan*. Food? Forget it. Only *prasad* would do. Krishnamurphy was hoping to cure them of their attachment to words and lead them to that precious moment before syllables were formed.)

'Right! Everyone, assume lotus position!' ordered Nasroodeen.

They all sat, dutifully. (They love anything with lotus in it.) Nasroodeen, the baskets still on his head, a virtual leaning tower of Pisa, began to move his head up and down and sideways. The disciples gulped, fearing the tower would come crashing down. The head-bobbing continued. If anything it got worse. Torture!

'He's a basket case, no doubt about it,' said a disciple under his breath.

Finally, after twenty minutes, Krishnamurphy asked:

'Kindly reveal the purpose of this exercise.'

'Simple!' said the wise fool. 'Even Nasroodeen nods.'

The ensuing groans scattered a cloud of crows.

'Eggcellent!' said Cook, to no one in particular.

It Is Your Will

It is Your will
That the snake ascends the tree
And steals an egg
It is Your will that another egg is spared
Spare not my poem
Rob the nest
Leave me empty in Your grace

A Quiet Stroll

Krishnamurphy took his followers for a contemplative stroll in the garden. Suddenly, Nasroodeen jumped out of the bushes, his face painted in grotesque colours, shaking a lethal-looking spear.

'Who the devil do you think you are?' said Krishnamurphy.

'Shakespeare!' came the blood-curdling reply.

Answers

As previously noted
Krishnamurphy does not compose riddles
But he's the smartest of all gurus
When it comes to clever answers:
Turf
A snail
A heron standing on one leg
A hedgehog
The *bodhrán*
(Goatskin drum)
A sea anemone.

How did I do?

In the Glasshouse

'As you know,' said Krishnamurphy, 'we mustn't live in the head all of the time. It's important to get out, do some pruning, digging, watering, weeding, that kind of thing. Helping Cook to peel the vegetables while assisting him with the intricacies of the English language. Though he prefers *mouna* – silence – to English. Thinks it might be better as a universal language ...

'Where was I? Oh yes, manual work. *Laborare est orare*, you know, to work is to pray. Such grounding activities are all highly praised by the Zen masters and the Chinese Patriarchs before them. That is why I propose we all go down to the glasshouse and get our fingernails dirty. OK? The Ayurvedic plants in particular need some serious attention. We must keep a constant supply of fresh brahmi – *bacopa monieri* – as I believe it is the only remedy for some of you! And/or sankapuspi – *convolvulus pluricaulis*. So then, come on, let's go.'

And off they went. Once inside the glasshouse they heard a strange whooping sound. What could it be? They were as puzzled as bedamned.

'It's only me!' said Nasroodeen and all of a sudden he starting throwing turnips at the disciples. One fat turnip after another!

'Ouch! Ouch!'

Each turnip found its mark.

Krishnamurphy became very animated.

'Nasroodeen! What the devil are you up to?'

'By the Beard of the Prophet! What does it look like? I am throwing turnips at your assassins!'

'I can see that but – why?'

'People in glasshouses shouldn't throw stones!'

Krishnamurphy stomped off, muttering a menacing mantra, and wasn't seen again until way after supper time.

Where Do We Start?

Krishnamurphy: We began our *satsang* this morning – as we have so often done before and as we shall in all likelihood do again – with the rhetorical question, 'Where do we start?'

We don't.

There is no beginning.

No end.

No curtain up on this drama.

No curtain down.

No producer.

No director.

This is No-Theatre.

It cannot be emphasised enough.

It is the key to what follows and what has gone before.

I ask you, 'Where do we start?'

Surmising a beginning or an end is a concept, an exercise of the mind, a projection in time and space, no more real than stage scenery.

Disciple: Excuse me! What's all that in plain

English?

Krishnamurphy:	Plain English cannot grasp it.
Disciple:	How then is it grasped?
Krishnamurphy:	It is not for the grasping. It grasps us.
Disciple:	What does?
Krishnamurphy:	The question – where do we start? All commencements, including our birth – what are they? They are not commencements at all. We invent commencements, stages. There is only one eternal Reality. Indivisible by nature.
Disciple:	I can gather that ... I think.
Krishnamurphy:	It's ungatherable. Better to watch Cook taking layers off an onion until nothing is left, better by far than all this musty wordiness.

Disciple:	I know where you're coming from.
Krishnamurphy:	I'm not coming from anywhere. I am not going anywhere.
Disciple:	You're a desperate man! A terrible man ... If you're not coming or going, are you static?
Krishnamurphy:	No, dynamic.
Disciple:	You're doing my head in ... I know, I know – forget the head, you say! But how? You are dynamic? Define, please.
Krishnamurphy:	By defining it you limit it. It is limitless.
Disciple:	What is?
Krishnamurphy:	The dynamic of the universe. It can only be intuited – and lived – by the Heart, the Heart informed by intelligence. And devotion. And surrender. Fused.

One.

Always.

Now.

Awake.

Disciple: You are at one with everything?

Krishnamurphy: This is the meaning of our opening gambit – where do we start?

We do not start at all.

Disciple: I'll start to get it one of these days.

Krishnamurphy: Don't start.

Surrender –

in the name of the Law!

Did I ever tell you about the time I enlisted in the army of Genghis Khan?

Disciple: No … I think we would have remembered that.

Krishnamurphy: It was a painful period in my life.

I was being shot all the time – by divine arrows.

But Genghis Khan had the answer.

If anyone can do it, Genghis can,
says I.

All his men wore these silk shirts,
you see?

So, when an arrow penetrated your
body, some of the silk would get in.

You follow?

Much easier to pull out the arrow
that way.

Yes, I learned a lot during my
years with Genghis Khan.

Dead Donkey

Word came to the Krishnamurphy Ashram that Nasroodeen's favourite donkey had collapsed and died. Krishnamurphy suggested to his disciples that they pop over and offer their commiserations.

'Nasroodeen is a pest! So is his donkey – or *was*,' said one of the disciples.

'Pet or pest, it matters not. Haven't we spoken long enough about unconditional compassion? Now is the time to put it into practice.'

They all nodded, somewhat reluctantly. Each was silently rehearsing how to express their condolences to Nasroodeen. Having filled themselves with kind thoughts, they were ill-prepared for what they saw when they arrived. There was the Mullah Nasroodeen, in a lather of sweat, whipping the poor dead animal.

'You there! Desist! What in God's name are you doing?' exclaimed an outraged English disciple.

'What does it look like?' said Nasroodeen.

The disciple approached him, about to snatch the whip from the Mullah's hand. But the Mullah was too deft for him.

'What kind of horrific behaviour is this? Explain yourself, sir!'

Nasroodeen looked at him.

'No use flogging a dead horse,' said he.

Fashion

Disciple: What should I be doing?

Krishnamurphy: Doing? What do you mean,
what should you be doing?
Scratching if you have an
itch, chanting if you are into
bhakti or devotional Advaita,
repairing the toilet if you have any
interest at all in this ashram.

Need I go on?

Disciple: I am not a sanitary engineer. I am
a seeker.

Krishnamurphy: Seek schmeek!

Seek your nose!

Wake up!

Disciple: I will not be insulted.

Krishnamurphy: Oh yes you will!

Seek, will you?

Put on a turban, then, be a proper
Sikh!

Disciple:	I'm really not sure what I'm doing here, listening to all this guff.
Krishnamurphy:	Then keep quiet. Best thing for you.
Disciple:	But surely –
Krishnamurphy:	Yes?
Disciple:	Seriously, what is it I should be doing? What should I do with my life?
Krishnamurphy:	Butcher? Baker? Candlestick maker? Your choice! You could be President of the United States of America! Or you could burn with truth. You could be me – up here – and I could be there listening to you. Does it matter what you do? Become a fashion designer for all I care.

The Dhammapada says:

'Engineers fashion wells,
carpenters fashion wood, the wise
fashion themselves.'

The Way to the Stars

'Your wretched followers are addling your brain! You need a break – mark my word – or they will suck you dry! Take my donkey,' said Nasroodeen to Krishnamurphy. 'Go out into the wilds at once, sit down and gaze at the brimming stars.'

'I think I might just do that,' said Krishnamurphy. 'Where are the nearest wilds?'

Half way to the nearest wilds, the donkey threw Krishnamurphy. He landed on his head, poor man, and immediately began to see stars!

When he returned he related what happened to Nasroodeen.

'*Sic itur ad astra,*' said Nasroodeen, laughing, 'such is the way to the stars!'

'Pretending to know Latin, now, are we? Bet you learned that from some book of quotations!'

'I'm not going to grace that with a reply, Krishnamurphyji!'

'Why not?'

'*Aquila non capit muscas!*'

'What?'

'An eagle does not catch flies ...'

Obscure Texts

Disciple: Why do you quote from obscure texts?

Krishnamurphy: For my own amusement.

But who says they are obscure?

I should quote from *The Wall Street Journal*?

Nothing is obscure to the clear eye.

Disciple: But, Master –

Krishnamurphy: I am not your master.

You must be your own master.

Nay, all of you, be rare priceless masterpieces ... unique manifestations of the One.

Disciple: Non-master ... koans are obscure texts, are they not? What is the sound of one hand clapping?

Krishnamurphy: A masterly riposte!

Aren't you the *gob naoscai!*

Disciple:	The what?
Krishnamurphy:	Literally a snipe's beak! Why can't you learn some Irish, or Latin, or Sanskrit – a sensible language. A *gob naoscaí* is someone far too inquisitive for his own good. Nevertheless, double rations of grog all round, ye salty mariners! And when ye are downing the grog, please remember – these satsangs are not to impress one another with novel arguments or ideas. We are not here to argue! Rid yourself of such words as satsang, darshan, karma and all the rest of it. Stop arguing – with me and with yourself. The *Psura Sutta* says, 'Disputation never leads to purity.'
Disciple:	You're quoting again – because you have no answer for the koan!
Krishnamurphy:	Let's have some music ... Leonard Koan, perhaps?

Jein, Says Krishnamurphy

There's a word in German
Not taught in schools.
The word in question is *Jein*.
It's a type of composite –
Ja and *Nein*.
Yes and No (Nes and yo).
Is this a poem?
Jein!

Explain the Mystery of the Trinity.
Jein! Jein! Jein!

The River

Krishnamurphy took his followers out on a ginko. They came in view of a river.

'Look, it's himself!' said Krishnamurphy, grinning from ear to ear.

Sitting on his donkey, perfectly still, was the sagacious Nasroodeen, his grey beard in disarray.

'Shhh … ' said Krishnamurphy, 'let's hide here and watch him for a while. I'm sure he'll afford us some amusement.'

They watched for over an hour. Nothing was happening.

'What ever is he doing?' asked one of the followers. 'Looks like he's in some kind of a trance – or a coma!'

'*Rusticus expectat dum defluat amnis* – he is waiting like some dull-witted bumpkin for the river to run by!' said Krishnamurphy, smiling.

The donkey brayed and cocked one ear. Nasroodeen turned the animal around and came at a fast trot to where Krishnamurphy and his followers were.

'Still hanging around, eh?' said Nasroodeen, fingering his beard. 'Nothing better to do, eh?' He eyed them severely. 'Dull-witted bumpkins!'

A Very Cold Day

The stove was lit. It was a dark, cold day outside. Soon the sky would fill with snow. The disciples were snug inside. And Cook had made them all some warm Nuffin' Muffins. (Nothing much in them but, at least, they were warm.)

Krishnamurphy was about to sing one of his rare evening bhajans when someone pointed to the window.

'Look outside! It's Nasroodeen!'

Krishnamurphy looked out.

'Hmmm ... so it is,' he remarked, nonchalantly. Then, taking a key from his pocket, he went to the door and locked it.

The disciples looked at each other in utter stupefaction.

'Now, come over here to the window,' said Krishnamurphy.

They all looked out. Snow was falling on Nasroodeen's head. It made him look like one of the ancients.

They watched and they watched and after a while, Nasroodeen's beard became icy and a drop from his nose turned into an icicle. He was a pitiful sight.

One of the disciples couldn't bear it any longer.

'For pity's sake, will you not let the poor man in?'

Krishnamurphy looked at him, straight in the eye, saying, *'Probitas laudatur et alget* – honesty is commended and left out in the cold.'

A Matter of Life and Death

Disciple: What happens to the soul after death?

Krishnamurphy: It travels First Class to Tibet!

Death, you say?

No such thing.

There is only life.

That's all ...

Disciple: But ... life leaves the body, does it not?

Krishnamurphy: So ...?

Why call it death?

It is still life, is it not, whether in the body or out of the body.

I am frequently out of my body – but I don't expect you to bury me each time, do I?

Disciple: When you are out of the body, are you a zombie?

Krishnamurphy: The previous offer regarding

double rations of grog has been
rescinded!

The Nesting Mullah

'I'm sorry to be interrupting your lecture,' said the new security guard to Krishnamurphy, 'but there seems to be a suspicious-looking character perching outside on a branch. Have a look for yourself,' said he, handing his binoculars to the sage.

Krishnamurphy went to the window.

'Ah, sure that's only Nasroodeen. He's away with the birds!'

The Odour of Sanctity

Disciple:	Who are you exactly? What are you?
Krishnamurphy:	You would like to know, wouldn't you?
	I am the Old Woman of Beare,
	I am the Salmon of Knowledge,
	I am Sancho Panza and the Baal Shem Tov.
	Nobody really.
	What does it say in the *Upasivamanava Puccha*?
Disciple:	I haven't the foggiest.
Krishnamurphy:	Let's dispel that fog, shall we?
	'Just as a flame that has become extinguished by the wind can no longer be identified, so the tranquil sage who is released from mind and body can no longer be identified.'
Disciple:	What about Cook? Who is he when he's at home?

Krishnamurphy:	He is at home in the universe.
	But, why don't you ask him?
Disciple:	You have forbidden us!
Krishnamurphy:	Oh, yes ... so I have.
	His methods are not for you.
	Not yet.
	When you are ready, he will give a seminar all about crows.
	It will change your life.
	Yes, you heard correctly.
	Crows.
	He lived with the crows once.
	Yes, he is a very holy man indeed.
	A Jain.
	He only eats oranges.
	I know he exudes a rather pleasant citric odour but I think you should stop sniffing him all the time!
	I know, it's hard.
	I do it myself.
	Unconsciously.
Disciple:	Some of us think he is more enlightened than you.

Krishnamurphy:	What's this then, a mutiny?
	He's Cook.
	He cooks, when he's not on strike or lost somewhere in his search for beneficial herbs.
	Cook. That is all.
	Let him cook!
	Nobody is more enlightened than the next.
	You are enlightened or not.
	Awake or asleep.
	What did you say when you got up this morning?
	'I am asleep?'
	Cook is awake.
Disciple:	What about the Buddha?
Krishnamurphy:	The Buddha is the Tathagata.
	He is beyond everything.
	Beyond enlightenment.
Disciple:	What is beyond enlightenment?
Krishnamurphy:	Omniscience.
Disciple:	What is beyond omniscience?

Krishnamurphy:	The ocean of compassion.
Disciple:	What lies beyond the ocean of compassion?
Krishnamurphy:	Nothing.
	The ocean of compassion is boundless, eternal.
Disciple:	You make the answers up as you go along.
Krishnamurphy:	You make the questions up as you go along.
Disciple:	We have come here for knowledge. You are not being reasonable!
Krishnamurphy:	Aurobindo says: 'What men call knowledge is the reasoned acceptance of false appearances. Wisdom looks behind the veil and sees ...'
	Mmm ... what's that pleasant odour?
	Ah, Cook!
	What's for dinner?

Cook: I thought we might be doing a three-day fast?

In a Jam

The ashram was plagued by bees. Krishnamurphy couldn't bear the thought of exterminating them. They were even in the kitchen and Cook, a pious Jain, would rather be stung a dozen times than do harm to any of God's creatures. (He even has difficulty chopping carrots).

Krishnamurphy called Nasroodeen for advice.

'I'm on my way!' said the trustworthy Mullah.

He arrived within the hour.

'You see?' he said to Krishnamurphy. 'We'll leave this pot of jam over here. The bees will come – if such be their karma – and they'll get stuck in the jam. It will be a sweet death! They may not even die. But, at least, they will be distracted. So, don't worry!'

'Jam? Is this the best you can do?'

'Believe me, I have thought about it, long and hard!'

'No you haven't! You were on your way before I had put down the phone!'

'My friend, I have thought about this before – in previous lives – many, many times. You called to say you were in a jam. The solution was already in your call! Jam it is. Trust me!'

'OK. Let's have a game of chess.'

'What I like best about chess,' said Nasroodeen, 'is when it's over.'

'When it's over? How come?'

'I get a chance to use an Italian proverb – when the game is over, the pawn and the king go into the same box.'

'You're a strange man,' said Krishnamurphy.

***

Nasroodeen set the jam-jar on the compound wall and the friends soon forgot all about it, engrossed as they were in their game.

After a while, a pair of busy bees found themselves in the jam.

The buzzing distracted the players.

'How many of them are caught?' asked Krishnamurphy, a little perplexed.

Nasroodeen went over to check the jam-jar and when he returned to his seat there was a deep solemnity in his eyes.

'How many are caught? It is difficult to say, Murph!'

'What man, can't you count?'

'It is not a matter of counting. It is a question of reality, really. A philosophical question.'

'Why don't you leave the philosophy to me, Nasroodeen? How many bees have been caught?'

'Maybe two, maybe not.'

'Maybe two, maybe not? Meaning?'

'Two bee … or not two bee …'

Krishnamurphy Has a Flea in His Ear

Beloved followers,

Stop following me around.

Today I am a Jain.

What? exclaim the incredulous disciples.

I have a flea in my ear,

I must extricate it – as only a Jain can –

With the utmost dexterity.

So leave me be.

Stop following me around!

Out of my Wei Wu Wei!*

(*Wei Wu Wei, sage, also known as 000. His father was High Sheriff of Armagh, Northern Ireland.)

The Evolution of a Flea

Disciple:	The other day, when you had a flea in your ear ... we were discussing it among ourselves ... and it appeared to some of us that you had lost your cool ...
Krishnamurphy:	Appeared, did it?
	Beware of appearances.
	Osho never lost his cool?
	Jesus?
	Finn Mc Cool?
	J Krishnamurti?
	U G Krishnamurti?
	Cook?
	Lost my cool, did I?
	Where did I lose it?
	Will you help me find it?
	All of you!
	Go look for it!
	Anyone who finds it will be rewarded – with sudden enlightenment!
Disciple:	Well, when you put it that way ...

though comparing Cook to Jesus is
a bit much.

Krishnamurphy: You might tell me why, sometime
                   ...
                   Discussing a flea in my ear, then,
                   were you?
                   Have you nothing better to
                   discuss?

Disciple: Well ...

Krishnamurphy: There was no flea!
                   There was no me!
                   There was no cool to lose ...

Disciple: Oh! Cool ... I get it.

Krishnamurphy: You get it or you think you get it?

Disciple: I think I get it ...

Krishnamurphy: Here's Cook.
                   I will ask him.
                   Cook, do you think they are
                   getting it?

Cook: Getting what?

Krishnamurphy:	The message.
Cook:	Massage is good.
Krishnamurphy:	No – message, message.
Cook:	Message? No, message no good. Massage very good.
Krishnamurphy:	Cook is quite right. Give yourselves an abhanga massage and take the rest of the day off.
Disciple:	May we not ask Cook a few questions?
Krishnamurphy:	Cook?
Cook:	They can be asking anything until the crows come home. But it is all a matter of *syadvad!*
Krishnamurphy:	Which is what?
Cook:	Relativity.

Krishnamurphy:	Oh, do you really think so?
Cook:	Relatively speaking. This is what we are being told.
	This, also, is what I am seeing and smelling and so forth.
Disciple:	He can smell relativity?
	Excuse me, Cook, who founded your religion?
Cook:	Perhaps you are hearing of the most famous one, Lord Mahavira?
Disciple:	Afraid not.
Cook:	Well, he was – how are you saying it in English?
	Top notch chap.
	Pukka.
	Also his mother top notch.
	Tip top!
	If all of you were having her for a mother you would not be here trying to find out about the meaning of life.
	You would be living your lives in the odour of sanctity.

Disciple: What did Mahavira do?

Cook: What did he not do?
         What is he not doing all the time?

Disciple: OK. What did he not do?

Cook: Nothing that he did not do.

Disciple: What does Jainism mean, exactly?

Cook: It is coming from 'jina' which is
         conqueror.
         We are conquering the woes.
         All the woes.
         Old woes.
         New woes.
         You are seeing me wearing a mask in the
         kitchen? This is not for hygienic purposes.
         No. Not at all.
         It is for keeping out the flies.
         A Jain is not swallowing a fly.

Disciple: What is your view of the universe?

Cook: It is coming and going.
         Now I am thinking it is going.

But it will be back.

Disciple: You believe in the transmigration of souls,
I believe?

Cook: Correct.

Very much.

There are many different categories, you
see.

The *nigoda* – these are without the senses,
you see? Then we have beings having
just the one sense – touch – and here
we are putting the stones, edible roots of
the tasty vegetables and such things, you
see? No touch.

Also there are beings with two senses –
touching and tasting, see? Tasting and
touching.

Our good friends the little pink worms
are crawling into this category.

Two senses.

Follow?

Good.

The candle-loving moths and the bug-
eyed bugs?

Two senses they are having, too – and a
third!

What is this?

Anyone guess?

No?

What?

Don't be silly.

Answer in front of nose.

Smelling!

Yes! Smelling it is.

And so it goes you see.

On and on.

Are we adding another sense?

Of course.

The wasp and the mosquito – also the wily scorpion, which we do not find here in Ireland but he is very much existing, did not Sai Baba step on him – all with sense of what?

Sight.

Of course.

And all of you people are belonging to the category of the five senses.

Disciple: Could I come back as a scorpion?

Cook: In your case I am thinking a goat.

Disciple: Thanks …

Cook:	Don't be thanking me.
	Be thanking your good self.
	Goat, pig, scorpion, human, what does it matter as long as you are awake?
Disciple:	What do you think of Krishnamurphy's Spiritual Anarchy?
Krishnamurphy:	You don't have to answer that!
Cook:	Is that what he is calling it now?
	It is just having a name.
	A new name.
	It is not my cup of chai.
	Then again, we mustn't be condemning because, as I say, it is all a matter of *syadvad*, relativity.
	What Krishnamurphy means, as far as I am gathering his methods, is that spiritual anarchy is the dynamic way:
	We must be bringing down the government of ego!
	We must be storming the bastions of lethargy, custom and habit.
	We must know ourselves to be awake and declare it with an overflowing heart.

But for me, you see, the storming
of bastions is a crude metaphor:

the supreme religion is non-
violence – *ahimsa parmo dharma*.

This is the crux.

The core.

The heart of the matter.

The centre.

The hinge.

All is hinging on this.

Yes, the core.

How are you having an apple
without a core?

And Tagore, he is saying it, too,
in a different way, 'There is
no higher religion than that of
sympathy for all that lives.'

This is what he is saying and this
is pure Jainism. Even though he is
a Bengali intellectual, always
painting and composing songs and
so forth and winning Nobel Prizes
with the help of Mr Yeats and all
that.

But he is immaculately correct in
this matter of sympathy.

Not so much God and ritual and
all that – which is often causing
violent headaches –

no, simply no more *himsa*, no

more violence.

Ever again.

Which is why we are not
swallowing the fly.

Disciple: This is the essence of your
scriptures?

Cook: We are having modern scriptures
as well as old scriptures you know.

With many old scriptures, people
are scratching their heads all of the
time or throwing them out with
the bathwater – not the heads, the
scriptures.

Sometimes I am feeling it would
be good to be throwing out the
heads too.

What is the meaning of this and
that?

Who is saying what?

Because a lot of these gods and
demons and treatises and sutras
and what are you having, all are
relating to another cultural
background, you see, and another
time.

We are adding to our scriptures.

The *Atma-Siddhi* by Shrimad
Rajchandra, for instance. He was
not a prophet in the wilderness,

wearing the loincloth and eating the locusts, you see.

Which is also bananas – because it was not locusts but carob.

Like chocolate.

Anyway, we mustn't criticise.

Shrimad Rajchandra was a successful jeweller.

Tops! But this did not matter.

He saw the most precious jewel of all!

Top notch fellow, hopped into the world in 1868. Taught Mahatma Gandhi all that is worth knowing. And hopped off again.

Understand what this hopping is all about.

Do not hop in if you don't know how to hop out.

So, you have come here, to this place, for Self-Realisation?

The *Atma-Siddha* says this:

Kashaay ni upashaant taa maatr moksh abhilaash

Bhave khed antar dayaa te kahiye jignaas:

You wish I am translating this shloka for you?

I will try.

But it is difficult.

I learned my English from an Irish nun, Sister Assumpta, and my syntax is not without sin.

But the heart is immaculate, in so far as I am seeing.

Sister Assumpta was teaching me a Christmas carol.

I am remembering this now.

Bitter sweet I am telling you.

Christmas carol, and it wasn't even Christmas.

'The first Noel the angels did say was to certain poor shepherds in fields as they lay ...'

And for a long time I am speaking English like that. Here is the shloka:

'One in whom passion has subsided, who is only desiring liberation,

For whom rebirth is sorrow, who is having compassion in his heart, he is the true candidate for Self-Realisation ...'

We must be awake to this.

Krishnamurphy: Thank you, Cook! That was pukka! Excellent translation too, I might add.

Cook: Ripe fruit, Krishnamurphy.
That is all.
Ripe fruit falling into my hands.
I am only passing it on again.

Krishnamurphy: Any more questions?

Cook: I am having one for you!
What is this Spiritual Anarchy of
yours?

Krishnamurphy: The heart is already brimful with
divine love, is it not?

Cook: Um.

Krishnamurphy: But it requires an act of
understanding and an act of will to
subvert the ego – and even
the biological identity itself – in
order to allow the heart to rule,
spontaneously, with loving
kindness.

Cook: Then I too am becoming a
spiritual anarchist ...

Disciple:	Cook, in my country –
Cook:	What is the country of your origin precisely?
Disciple:	The United States of America.
Cook:	I have heard of it. But it is not your country.
Disciple:	I beg your pardon?
Cook:	Do you own it?
Disciple:	No ... of course not.
Cook:	It will be very good to own less and less. And less. Be like Mahavir. He is ending up with nothing. Not even the cloak on his back. Naked as a frog. You have a question?
Disciple:	Well, yes ... as a matter of fact.

Cook:	Matters of fact are not always matters of fact.
Disciple:	That relates to my question actually. In my country – that is to say, in the USA, there is a raging debate going on between creationists and evolutionists. What is your stand on this?
Cook:	There are too many raging debates going on.
	People are not learning anything from debates.
	Silence is needed.
	Anyway, one group is looking to science, no?
	The other is looking to Judaeo-Christian scriptures, yes?
	It is my belief that both science and scripture are evolving.
	Or should.
	They may well evolve to the point of almost meeting. And then they are going their separate ways again. Perhaps.
	Who knows?
	You are a Christian?

Disciple:	Yes …
Cook:	You must read Teilhard de Chardin. He was a priest – a Jesuit – but he also knew a thing or two about evolution.
	He could see something spiritual in evolution.
	Top notch!
Disciple:	I see. So neither science nor scripture are fully developed at the moment?
Cook:	What matters science?
	What matters scripture?
	What matters is the eternal soul – not the karmic vehicle it may have now, or might have had in the past.
	Many creationists are racists.
	They cannot conceive of an immortal soul occupying a hairy ape.
	It is a cosmetic argument they are having.
	The evolution of a jaw-bone is of no great significance.
	What matters is the ascent of the soul. This is a cosmic matter – not cosmetic.

Disciple:	But the soul of an ape – if it has a soul – is not the soul of a human, surely?
Cook:	You are knowing this? For a fact?
	You have seen the soul?
	You are seeing enough souls to be comparing them all?
	Suppose there is only one soul.
	Then this one soul is in everything.
	Hairy ape too.
	Ape's brain is different.
	Surely.
	But ape's spirit?
	How different?
	You have seen ape's spirit?
Disciple:	No ...
Cook:	Of course not ...
	When soul is occupying man, so to speak ... or when man is occupying soul when man is ensouled at birth ... the greatest longing is for the soul to awaken to its own divine intelligence, its timeless origin in divine love – limitless, undivided love that was shining forth before

dinosaurs were plodding through the thickets and roaring their heads off all over the place.

All the *himsa* – the violence – all the sorrow of this world is coming about through the frustration or the neglect of Self-Realisation as soul. In such a state of frustration and neglect, how is it possible to see the soul in another?

Impossible, except fleetingly in a smile, in a bride's kiss, a mother's embrace, in the echoes of a poem.

So, external wars, internal wars, all of these are boiling down to one thing: a lack of utilising the spontaneous creativity of the awakened soul – the soul awakened to itself.

The soul was not created – the creationists are stuck in a time warp about this and the very concept of the soul is meaning little, of course, to a lot of the evolutionists.

Now, once you understand that the soul is ever-existent, then your life is changed utterly – the focus, the meaning, the intensity of your life suffers a sea-change. You become the ocean that you always were and always will be.

Krishnamurphy: Seaweed-flavoured Ocean Soup for lunch then, Cook?

Cook: It will be giving me the rarest of earthly pleasures.

Krishnamurphy's Last Will and Testament

Krishnamurphy has made his last will and testament.

Left everything to the poet Hafiz.

'Who is this Hafiz?' his lawyers beg to know.

'My brother,' says Krishnamurphy.

'Last known address, please?'

'Don't know the exact address but he died in 1518.

Might that be of some help to you?'

Keepers of the Word

Disciple:

Why is it nobody attends your
Friday satsangs?

Krishnamurphy:

Might it have something to do
with the fact that Friday talks are
conducted entirely through the
medium of Irish?

Disciple:

Precisely! Nobody understands
that language! You're just being
your anarchic self again!

Krishnamurphy:

You're free to leave at any time if
you dislike my methods. This is an
ashram. Not a gulag.

Daily talks are for the benefit
of those who are present – in
the here and now – and possibly

for the sake of some wayward soul
in the future.

Friday talks are for generations
past.

Disciple:

And you seriously think they are
listening?

Krishnamurphy:	Who is to say – seriously or not – that they are not?
Disciple:	Why can't you provide a translation?
Krishnamurphy:	How would you translate the word *ullastráth*?
Disciple:	I haven't a clue.
Krishnamurphy:	'The day before the day before yesterday!'
Disciple:	And this word, *ullastráth* - or whatever you call it – this is supposed to convey some valuable wisdom?
Krishnamurphy:	Not at all, not in itself. It's the way I say it!

A Talk in Irish for Generations Past
(Short Extract from a Five-Hour Sermon)

Tánn sibh ann, a dhaoine uaisle. Bhur gcéad fáilte! Is deas bheith ag caint libh arís. Conas tánn sibh ó shin? Tá cúrsaí ag dul chun donais anseo, mar is gnáth, cúrsaí áirithe ar aon nós, agus cúrsaí eile ag dul i bhfeabhas. Nach in mar a bhíonn i gcónaí. Ní gá dhom é sin a mhíniú daoibhse. Tuigeann sibhse go maith. Tuigeann sibh go rímhaith. Rómhaith a thuigeann sibh ....

Cuid eile agaibh is ag ligint oraibh atánn sibh go dtuigeann sibh an bladar seo. Bladar. Sea. Nach bhfuil an ceart agam?

Sea, cad tá le déanamh in aon chor? Meabhraím daoibh an rann druileála a bhí ag na hÉireannaigh Aontaithe. Ní cuimhin libh é? Is uaibhse a d'fhoghlaimíos é:

Cuir cos do phíce le barr do spáige,

Tomhais as sin go dtí do bhásta:

Tabhair truslóg ar aghaidh, agus déan sáthadh –

Léim ar gcúl agus bí ar do gharda.

Krishnamurphy relives his days in the Zoo

I am in charge of the monkeys!
'You have a natural way with them,'
I was told. Yes, of course I have,
I will take care of them for ever and a day.
Overtime? No problem.
I will stick close, day and night.
What's to go home to? Beans? Television?
I want to be with them always
Take care of their every need
Mind them in autumn
When leaves begin to scatter
Like dreams of youth
Mind them in wintertime
As they look out through their bars at the rude frost
Tell them little harmless stories
Recite great poems
Open up the world of myth –
Hanuman!
The monkey god!
We will greet this god playfully in the morning
And also at dusk, shadow-wrestling time,
For him only will we play hide and go seek

Chew nuts in his honour
As we natter deep deep into the night ...

Dawn! Chattering mind ceases.

Baffling Behaviour

It was a difficult morning. Had all of the sannyasins got out on the wrong side of the bed? Nothing seemed to be penetrating. Have I overworked them? thought Krishnamurphy to himself.

The disciples were sitting around, cross-legged and disgruntled.

The door flung open and Nasroodeen appeared with a shovel. He tossed the contents into the centre of the room. Foul-smelling stuff. There was immediate consternation.

'You filthy swine!' exclaimed a girl from Australia. 'How dare you desecrate this ashram!' The others were too shocked to open their mouths. Cook came in, to discuss the menu with Krishnamurphy, spotted the foul mess and slid off again quietly.

Krishnamurphy composed himself.

'What is the meaning of this?'

Nasroodeen looked at Krishnamurphy and winked at him:

'If you can't dazzle them with brilliance,' he cackled, 'baffle them with bullshit!'

(From the) Private Diaries of Krishnamurphy

There's nowt so quare as folk, as they say. A Finnish disciple – she must have been nearly seven foot tall, I seemed to be staring at her navel much of the time – she says, 'Krishnamurphyji …'

'Next you will be calling me Bhagwan! Drop the *ji* bit. Drop everything!'

'OK. I just wanted to ask, is it true you haven't defecated in ten years?'

Oh, shit. What does one say? They enquire about bowel movement instead of the music of the spheres?

But it was clear that she wouldn't stay much longer in our midst if I denied having such retentive, yogic powers. And she really needs to stay. She hasn't even found out what brought her here.

So, I nodded. (What is a nod? It could mean anything).

She just opened her mouth and silently mouthed a 'Wow!'

I'll give her a wow if it's a wow she's after … she won't know what hit her!

* * *

The Germans ask questions about defecation, too – as well as everything else – politics, sex, diet, the environment. I'm supposed to know everything? Please! 'How will George W. Bush be remembered?' asks a Siemens employee from Munich.

'Memory is a living thing,' I inform him. 'The awakened ones will put his memory to sleep – so that children don't have nightmares.'

One makes it up as one goes along. So many questions. We need silence ... My work here is preparing them for silence, but first we have to answer a lot of silly questions.

* * *

Stuffed nose yesterday. Asked the Mullah Nasroodeen to take over the satsang. He agrees, as long as it is held outside. He feels confined within four walls. I sit and listen. German disciple stands up and clears his throat somewhat ostentatiously, I thought.

'Mullah,' says he, ' I have failed to get a satisfactory answer from Krishnamurphy on the precise meaning of the sound of one hand clapping.' He looks at me, rather accusingly.

'Perhaps, Mullah, you might elucidate, kind Sir?'

Was there a hint of irony in 'kind Sir'?

I am supposed to solve their koans for them? It's not koans they want. It's ice-cream koans ...

Anyway, the Mullah stood up, turned around, leaned over and farted.

Then he got on his donkey and – before riding away – the donkey farted too!

I must have him over again soon ...

* * *

Weather has changed for the good so we talk a while on the Way of the White Cloud. But all of the sannyasins are still rooted in a false sense of identity. Except for one. The Canadian girl. She is on the brink. But when I questioned her, she had only been moving with the white cloud in a kind of stupor.

'You are still attracted to the pleasures of idle dreaming!' I tell her, with a mixture of kindliness and severity which she so badly needs. I stroke her hair, gently. She looks up.

I say, 'The white cloud will darken, love – and will fall as rain!'

She nodded. But what is a nod?

'I am not at the rain-stage, yet,' she says, sweetly.

'My love, how often have I said it? There are no stages!'

A look of fear comes into her eyes. I grab the moment.

'The rain will evaporate and become the white cloud again. It's a cycle! You are part of a cycle – NOW! – the white cloud ... darkening ... the rain – and, again, the white cloud, my fair one!'

She flashed a heavenly smile – like the bright sun coming out from a cloud.

* * *

The German disciple is very logical, very scientific in his thinking. Nevertheless, he's an excellent Ayurvedic student, I'll give him that and, with the help of some powders and oils, he has cleared up my stuffed nose completely.

'Clear thinking involves open eyes, open ears – also

open nose,' I informed him.

He looked at me; for a second I believed he was about to make a breakthrough but … he shrank back.

'Sure,' he said and excused himself.

I called him back.

'By *sure* I take it you think I was only amusing you, patronising you, right?'

'Whatever,' he said and marched off with his Ayurvedic vials.

Ah, these seekers! So near, yet so far away!

★ ★ ★

The Mullah came to see me. We passed a pleasant hour and a half talking about matters of which he knows absolutely nothing – astrology, reincarnation, Tantric sex, etc.

When, eventually, he rose to leave, he said, 'By the way, I've bought a new donkey. I was thinking of calling him Murph!'

I wagged a finger at him.

'Don't you dare!'

'Come, come, dear fellow!' says he. 'What's in a name?'

I took his point.

★ ★ ★

The German has left. Off to India.

'Believe me,' I say, 'there is nothing in India that is not here, you know.'

'Except fresher mangoes. I'll send you some,' he said.

* * *

The Canadian girl tells me, 'Krishnamurphy, I used to dream of you a lot. Even before I ever heard of you. Now I no longer see you in my dreams.'

'Excellent!' I cry. 'Best news I've heard in a week of Sundays!'

'Everything is clear now, undisturbed. Sometimes I feel as if I'm not even breathing.'

'When do you leave?'

'Noon tomorrow.'

'Go with the white cloud!'

I love it when they are ready to leave, when it clicks for them, when the Nothing Soup takes effect. There's something in the soup. No doubt about it.

* * *

My press secretary hands me a clipping from *The Sunday Reporter*. My God, they really have developed the art of misquoting to an unbelievable degree. Hold on ... this looks like something I might have said:

'I put it to you, Krishnamurphy, that you are brainwashing your followers!'

'Stuff and nonsense! They must wash their own brains!'

* * *

'What about urination?' asks the Finnish student, the one with the navel.

'What about it?'

'Do you urinate? Nobody has ever seen you urinating.'

'What is it with you, with your defecation and your urination? You see me laugh. You see me cry. You see me walking, standing, sitting, eating, drinking. Do you not? Sometimes I have a smoke. And you ask me do I urinate? Lucky for you Nasroodeen isn't standing in for me today – he would piss on you! And so would his donkey!'

★ ★ ★

The Heart of the Universe

Get to the heart of the universe, says Krishnamurphy,
By hook or by crook! Or Cook.

How? ask the trembling disciples.

Understand, says Krishnamurphy,
Understand that you are not the heart of the universe
And the heart of the universe will beat loudly in you!

Open!

'Open! Open!'
the dentist says to Krishnamurphy.
'Believe me, I could not be more open!'
whispers Krishnamurphy.

The dentist experiences samadhi.

Krishnamurphy discourses on Advaita

Not two,
Simply that,
Not two
This is the meaning of Advaita.
The hen? The egg?
No, not two.
Egg is extension of hen, no?
Everything extension of God, see? Of the One,
Ourselves included.
Myself and Saddam Hussein
Closer than brothers, OK?
Not a whit of difference between us
None at all
Couldn't possibly be. Ever. See?
Arabic is Gaelic, yes?
Gaelic is Arabic
In disguise.
Every vowel and consonant
Every sibilant is God's breath. Fine?
No language ever died
Or ever will
No person or wren has perished.
When you understand all this

And really it is all very simple
You will understand the nature of all things
Every colour
Every form

Cock a doodle doooo!
Hey! Did you not hear?
I am calling you!

Krishnamurphy in Love

I'm in love!
Yes, I'm in love!
In love, says K.

Who is she? The disciples ask, nervously.

Over there in the corner – see!

A cat? exclaim the startled disciples.

Yes, and the other one – look!

The cat was staring at a mouse.

What bird just flew by, eh? asks K.

A tit!

My beloved one!

Is there no one whom you do not love?

No, none at all.

What about the devil?

He most of all – if he exists –
Is in need of love.

The disciples did a little dance of joy
And soon were joined
By the cat, the mouse, the tit
And Old Nick himself
Nimbly on cloven hooves!

Belief

Disciple:

At school I felt very fortunate that most of my teachers believed in me. They also said, over and over again, 'Believe in yourself!' Now, you seem to be saying the opposite ...

Krishnamurphy:

Those who come to me and who believe in themselves, these are the people I have most difficulty with.

Your teachers were right when they said, 'Believe in yourself'.

They were preparing you for this world, a very competitive world.

But look here – this is not the London School of Economics, you know.

We are not trying to make better business men and business women out of you.

We are trying to shift the focus of your beliefs, we are trying to coax you to question the nature of belief itself, to see what vista remains when all edifices and constructs of the mind come tumbling down. This is Spiritual Anarchy, if we must give it a name.

We are plumbing the nature
of consciousness so that you
may live your lives free of the past,
uncoloured by the conditioned
mind.

Spiritual Anarchy is the basis of
this ashram – we will bring
down the government of false
reasoning, the corrupt government
of waffle and self-importance –
and spin!

We will storm the gates of
convention and belief.

Jesus was a good little boy who
obeyed his parents?

No, he wandered off and when
they caught up with him he said,

'I must be about my Father's
business.'

He was expressing freedom from
conventionality – putting his
spontaneous nature into action
and words.

We are not talking about beliefs
here.

You might as well believe in a
donkey!

The Mullah was training his
donkey last year – for the Donkey
Derby.

I jest not.

He really believed in that donkey!

But the donkey didn't know that –
nor did he care.

Dug his heels in at the start he did
– didn't compete at all! Wouldn't
budge.

Disciple: Did the Mullah's relationship to
the donkey change in any way
after that episode?

Krishnamurphy: He loves him all the more!

Anyway, how did we get to this?

Yes, it's fine if teacher says,
'Believe in yourself' but it would
be better to say 'Believe in and
know your Self'.

Koan

Disciple:	What is the sound of one hand clapping?
Krishnamurphy:	You will hear the sound of one hand slapping if you're not careful!
Disciple:	I ask you again, what is the sound of one hand clapping?
Krishnamurphy:	This is a koanspiracy!

★ ★ ★

Krishnamurphy Nearly Has a Kitten!

Disciple:
> What is the meaning of your haiku:
> a suppurated eye –
> the kitten does not scamper
> after blown leaves

Krishnamurphy:
> Haiku does not attempt to adorn.
> It sees things as they are.
> This is part of your training here.
> To see things simply as they are.
> To see yourselves as you are.
> This in itself is a revelation.

Disciple:
> You have a haiku about a cat ...

Krishnamurphy:
> Which one?

Disciple:
> from what unknown
> universe
> beyond Hubble –
> the cat's green stare

Krishnamurphy:
> What about it?

Disciple:	Things as they are? Surely not!
Krishnamurphy:	Why not?
	This, too, is things as they are – or as I see them. There is something older than all of us, older than time itself, in the cat's stare.
	Ultimately, things are as they are as a result of the Big Bang, no?
	In haiku we are in time but also outside of time; in space, but also outside of space.
	This is where I hope to bring you – all of you!
Disciple:	I knew it! Another bloody flying saucer cult!
Krishnamurphy:	Look, here comes Cook.
	See?
	He has an orange in his hand.
	Oh look, he's about to peel it.
	Now, there's a realized man if ever there was.
	Let's call him over and ask him what he is doing, shall we?
	Hello, Cook!
	What are you peeling there?

Cook:	A mystery.
Krishnamurphy:	See? Thank you, Cook, you may go.
Cook:	Like the previous Cook?
Krishnamurphy:	What do you mean? I didn't sack her, you know. She left. A pity. She was quite a good Cook.
Cook:	She was a good Cook, as Cooks go; and as good Cooks go, she went.
Krishnamurphy:	Saki?
Cook:	No thanks, I don't drink.
Krishnamurphy:	No, I mean Saki. He wrote that!
Cook:	He did?
Krishnamurphy:	You see, my friends? He even knows things he doesn't know!

Krishnamurphy Visits the Sick

'The sun has just come in the window', the old man sighs,

'Or is it I that have crept out

To greet it one last time?'

'It is both,' says Krishnamurphy, 'and both are one.'

'Ah! How it warms these old bones of mine!'

'I should turn all thoughts to the divine, should I not?

But what a pagan I've become! For me, today, the sun is God!'

'Since the sun was once created it, too, will die, my friend!

Aye! Ten million suns would not be God!' said the sage.

'But what could be brighter than the sun's rays?'

'Not your thoughts – whether they linger on the worldly or the divine.

What shines within! Uncreated! Indestructible!

Its light will shine beyond all days, beyond all space and time.'

Born Again

The Mullah paid Cook a surprise visit.

'I was thinking of becoming a Jain ...'

'No Mullah,' said Cook, 'bad idea. Anyway, that turban suits you down to heaven!'

'Down to the ground I believe is the expression. Heaven isn't down, is it?'

'It is.'

'Let's not get into that.'

'Into Heaven?'

'No, I mean. Where was I? Yes, I was thinking of becoming a Jain.'

'You might as well think of becoming a rooster. Anyway, a true Jain would never ride a donkey – lest he might be tempted to give it a kick or a whack or some such rude encouragement. And where would you be without your donkey?'

'Well, maybe I should become a vegetarian or – like your good self – a fruitarian.'

'No, you might as well become a kangaroo. You are an omnivore. I see you are eating everything. Also, you are saying everything that comes into your head. Myself, on the other foot, I am truly focussed on cooking and how best to practise ahimsa.'

'On the other hand ... not foot.'

'Do I care?'

'Ahimsa, you say. Hmmm ... What good is non-violence when someone hits you over the head?'

'Before this someone is hitting me over the head, I am saying: "Mr Someone, I have nothing. You are squeezing nothing out of me – except perhaps a few drops of orange juice." '

Nasroodeen adjusted his turban, bowed to Cook and departed, walking backwards, whereupon he bumped into Krishnamurphy.

'I have made a fantastic discovery, Krishnamurphy!'

'Another one? What is it this time, Nasroodeen?'

'I am delirious with joy.'

'We have known this for some time.'

'Oh, Krishnamurphy! Wait until you hear! I am a Muslim! A Muslim!'

Krishnamurphy looked at him and blinked rapidly.

'Excellent, my dear fellow, but I think we already – '

'Yes, of course, but now I am a born-again Muslim!'

Worst kind, thought Krishnamurphy to himself as the Mullah rushed off to share this incredible news with his donkey.

The Nothing Soup

Disciple: I have been displaying spontaneous mudras recently. Is this evidence of kundalini, or higher powers of some sort?

Krishnamurphy: What kind of spontaneous mudras? Show me.

Disciple: Like this.

Krishnamurphy: You have just consciously shown me these hand gestures, so how could they be spontaneous?

They are twitches, sir, spasmodic nothings.

Or worse, the craven machinations of ego.

We do not encourage so-called higher powers here. Your ordinary powers will do nicely.

Disciple: What about Cook?

Krishnamurphy: What about him?

Disciple:	Three weeks ago he served a soup. I scooped a spoonful of the same soup, put it into a container and sent it off to a friend of mine who works in a university laboratory. This morning he texts me to say there was nothing in the soup.
Krishnamurphy:	Nothing?
Disciple:	Absolutely nothing. No vitamins, minerals, proteins, fibres … nothing at all. No taste! (This much we knew already). No colour. Like distilled water, my friend informs me. No fats, no sodium, potassium.
	Nothing. What do you make of that?
Krishnamurphy:	His soup is well known in esoteric circles.
	It is a teaching device. Not for nothing is it called the Nothing Soup.
	Indeed, it is a teaching in itself.
	Some disciples come for nothing else.
	Seems they can't get enough of the Nothing Soup!

Haiku

Disciple: What is the meaning of your haiku:

> form is emptiness
> emptiness form –
> the half-moon slips from a cloud

Krishnamurphy: It's all in the Diamond Sutra.

Disciple: Which is what?

Krishnamurphy: The oldest book we know of, with a date.
It was found in the Caves of the Thousand Buddhas.

Disciple: Which are where?

Krishnamurphy: In China.

Disciple: Fine. But what is 'Form is emptiness, emptiness form'?

Krishnamurphy:	The truth, the whole truth and nothing but the truth.
Disciple:	It seems to make a mockery of the truths we are familiar with.
Krishnamurphy:	It does, rather, doesn't it?
	Then again, it may be the only truth there is.
Disciple:	You are not being very helpful.
Krishnamurphy:	Well, I try to be helpful – when I can.
	But certain hurdles you must jump for yourself, with no coaching from me.
	If the essence of the Diamond Sutra is nonsense to you, you have two choices.
	Ignore it.
	Or penetrate it – even if it takes all your life.
	My giving an explanation, a gloss, a lecture or a talk about it is no substitute for the power of the sutra to transform our whole notion of reality – and our behaviour subsequent to gaining that insight.

Disciple:	It's that important then, is it?
Krishnamurphy:	For some it is a matter of importance, yes.
	A matter of urgency.
	Once they have penetrated it, however, it doesn't seem to be all that important after all.
	Simply a law of the universe.
	Something that was quite obvious all along.
	But we become confused and befuddled – by our senses, let us say, and by what it says in the newspapers or on Fox News – now, there's a fox if ever there was one – and we miss the point of it all, the very essence of existence, of life.
Disciple:	Our behaviour ... Is our behaviour somehow superior to our thinking?
Krishnamurphy:	You are playing with ideas now.
	The Diamond Sutra is so called because it cuts through illusion.
	It says,
	'Buddhas are called Buddhas because they are free of ideas.'
	Now, once free of ideas, our

behaviour becomes very beautiful indeed.

It is a very radical notion, is it not, to be free of ideas.

It is hard to imagine Spiritual Anarchy without being attracted to the notion of being free of ideas. If you are attracted to the notion of being free of ideas, you are attracted to Freedom. If you are attracted to Freedom, you are awakening to a realization of your true Nature and Destiny.

Ah, ideas! We say 'I haven't an idea' in such a negative way; dismissive almost. 'I haven't a notion! I haven't a clue!'

Disciple:
I have had ideas all my life. In fact, I like to call myself an ideas man. Sometimes I have fifty or a hundred ideas a day.

Krishnamurphy:
That's a lot ... do you need that many?

Disciple:
How am I to stop having ideas – even though I may not be thoroughly convinced it's such a good idea to have so many ideas in the first place!

Krishnamurphy:	Of course you are not convinced!
	You probably had some very good ideas in your day. There's probably a few ideas buzzing around in your head at the moment.
	But what are your ideas?
	How to make a new product, let us say?
	Is it?
	How truly substantial is this idea of yours in the first place? How substantial, exactly, is the product?
	Is it everlasting?
	No.
	Is it as beautiful as a bunch of bananas?
	The Diamond Sutra gives us the following:
	All composed things are like a dream,
	A phantom, a drop of dew, a flash of lightning:
	That is how to meditate on them,
	That is how to observe them.
	So, you see, the sutra cuts through all things, all ideas, all phenomena, all achievements, all desires, the dreams and hopes of humanity.

It does not dash our hopes.

It just says it as it is.

Humanity will continue to dream, to hope, to achieve this or that or the other.

But it will never be at peace,

the world will never be without war and want until the light and the grace of the Diamond Sutra shines through all of us, through every pore, and to the farthest reaches of the universe. And when we truly understand that form is emptiness, emptiness form – then there is nothing to fight for or to defend and we begin to love one another and greet each day with a diamond-flashing smile.

Disciple:	I fear that all this might lead to passive inactivity.
Krishnamurphy:	Not at all!
	We will still need shelter and food and bridges across rivers.
	Soap.
	Incense.
	Education.
	The arts.
	The sciences.

Well, the essentials.

Water!

And the essentials are basically enough.

Where is the inactivity there?

The Buddha didn't say go into a cave and contemplate your navel.

No, he did enough of that himself to know it leads nowhere.

In his *Karaniya Metta Sutta* he admonishes us to be capable!

The spiritual life dull, inactive?

No, no, no.

It's exciting – though it does attract the occasional oddball ...

Cook! Where are you going? I didn't mean you!

Cook: You are inspiring me, Krishnamurphy, with all this talk of excitement! Tonight you are no longer going to be a guru, you will be a gourmet!

Krishnamurphy: What on earth do you intend dishing up, oh noble Jain?

Cook: Vegetarian duck – with orange sauce.

Krishnamurphy: What, pray, is vegetarian duck?

Cook: The sauce is easy.

The duck is the difficult part.

But I am working on it. I am not ducking the issue. I am a real cook. Not a quack! Namaste!

What Does Krishnamurphy Know?

I know the past
I know the present
And I know the future
But I will not utter
Its essence.
I have seen it
And trembled,
Tasted it
And swooned.
But it is of no avail.
Its essence
Is the purest silence
Imaginable.
Indeed, imagining it
Is to give a dream structure
To a reality
That cannot take form
Or words.
What is left?
When the embrace of words
And thoughts cools –
The blue icicle of Self –
              A fire roars.

The Guru Business

Disciple: How on earth did you get into the guru business?

Krishnamurphy: Oh ... well, in my green and salad days I used to read a lot of poetry.

Not just Rumi, Kabir, Hafiz, Mirabai and so on ...

I used to read everything.

There was a poem by a minor poet called Rex Taylor, though why he should be called minor – he's completely forgotten now – is another question.

A line or two touched me:

Even the wind is lost today
Or what it seeks cannot be found

Well, my friends, I too was totally lost.

Like the wind.

Floating, as it were, in a universe which seemed limitless and cold ... purposeless.

Anxious.

Violent.

Verbose.

Belligerent.

Rapacious.

Disciple: Then what happened?

Krishnamurphy: After what seemed aeons, the universe took pity on me ... it opened up and embraced me.

Disciple: And now?

Krishnamurphy: I'm still like the wind.

But not lost.

When such a thing happens, nothing is ever the same again.

So, I share this embrace with all of you and with all sentient beings.

Unconditionally.

That's all we're doing here.

That's what we're here for.

To find this out.

That's the sum of it.

Disciple: How did the universe embrace you? Was it like Da Free John in the Vedanta Temple in California

	– the embrace and effulgence of the eternal divine, the Shakti force?
Krishnamurphy:	Nothing quite as dramatic as that. From birth it was as if my arms were extended to embrace the universe. But I didn't believe my puny arms were wide enough.
Disciple:	And are they?
Krishnamurphy:	Yes, just right, in fact.

The universal embrace – the melting in one – teaches us this remarkable truth.

You see, in a way that is almost impossible for us to imagine, the universe is conscious of itself – in the bleating of a lamb, the roaring of a lion, in the destructive force of a volcano or a tsunami, in all the tender and violent acts of man.

And we – all of us – are that mystery of light and dark. Nothing more than the ego separates us from that consciousness, that ultimate experience.

The guru business is nothing more than helping you to discover the guru within – that which leads from darkness to brilliant light, unending. Live in that light and all of human history will be seen as nothing more than 'a buffalo's breath in winter' as a Native American poet once said: all oral and written literatures, all scriptures, testify to this.

Generation after generation, the guru business re-establishes the Diamond Sutra, cutting through illusion. The end of confusion, the end of misery, the end of rage and conflict, the re-emergence of serenity, peace, wisdom, love and silence – the lion, indeed, will lie down with the lamb!

The same heart that beats in both beats in you ... Listen.

And hear!

Disciple: Can one become a Self-realized being through poetry?

Krishnamurphy: Depends on the poetry.

Ramana Maharshi assures us that there are four paths to Self-realization.

Firstly, Self-enquiry, secondly *bhakti* – the path of devotion –

thirdly, service to mankind and, fourthly, pursuit of beauty.

Perhaps the true poet can walk all four paths simultaneously.

These will be the poets of the future.

Satsang with Cook

Disciple: I am unclear about your Nothing Soup...

Cook: You are speaking correctly.
The soup is clear.
It is your mind that is unclear.

Disciple: I see.

Cook: Nothingness is the goal of creativity.
So says Shonyo.

Disciple: Who he?

Cook: A Nobody.
A Nothing ...

Disciple: I see! Yes, now I see! Thank you!

Cook: De nada...

Dear Murph ...

(A short selection from the intimate and revealing correspondence between Krishnamurphy and Cook. No dates or addresses are given).

Dear Cook,

We miss you ... I am looking over some correspondence and here before me is your first ever letter to me. Do you remember? I quote:

'I would like to be applying for a job as your Cook. I am only willing to prepare pure *sattvic* food. I am having no previous experience. I am eating very little (oranges only) and am sleeping hardly at all. I will also be sweeping the ashram for you, morning and night. Noon also. I am in need of no salary as I am having no needs, obligations, attachments and such manner of things. I am a quick learner and soon I will be familiar with all your exotic Irish vegetables and seaweeds.

I am requiring three weeks annual leave to do a little sweeping in a small temple in India. The ticket will be paid by an Anonymous Benefactor. I am enclosing a photo of myself bathing in Gangotri, the source of the Ganges, for hygiene and sundry other purposes.'

You got the job, of course ...

Yours for ever,
Krishnamurphy

Dear Cook,

I like the cut of your jib, as they say. You have the job! Our neighbour, Nasroodeen, is doing the cooking at the moment but he never turns up and when he does he hasn't a clue and makes a song and dance about everything. He dances rather well, actually, and his singing is quite soothing but cooking is not his real vocation.

Come as soon as you can! We hunger for you.

Krishnamurphy

Dear Krishnamurphy,

Greetings from the Deerpark in India! I am enjoying my break. It is wonderful to know I am breathing the same air as Mahavira and the Buddha! I am not breathing in the flies, of course. I am wearing the compulsory mask as I sweep outside the Jain temple. And sometimes inside. Mostly I am sweeping. Sometimes not sweeping. Also sleeping. But also not sleeping. Quite a bit, actually.

When I am not sweeping I stand still. Some tourists come up to me and think I am one of those Hindu ascetics who is standing on one leg and letting his nails grow long and curvy for many years like the talons of some mythical bird. Then I go sweeping – or weeping! I am not one of your self-torturing sadhus, I say, curtly, and I am showing them my well-trimmed nails. They are disappointed.

I reminded them that Kabir had no time for ascetics, with their beards resembling that of a goat. Looking for wonders they are, these spiritual tourists. What is a wonder? The whole thing is a wonder. Everything!

I hope Nasroodeen is cooking up something nice for you all in my absence. Tell him to use a little turmeric. It will add a touch of yellow and brighten up the day for you all. It is important, in my absence, that he serves *sattvic* food only – cereals, fruit and vegetables and so on – so that your disciples are keeping their minds on higher things. No *rajasic* dishes such as fish, eggs, etc. and definitely no *tamasic* foods, such as my pet goat!

Your humble Cook

Dear Cook,

Please come back soon! Nasroodeen concocted some kind of a purgative and added it to the food. I believe he was reading a book in the library about *panchakarma* and got it into his head that we should all be purged! For our sins …. Anyway, we are all suffering from acute diarrhoea. The fact that it is yellow does not cheer us up one bit. He probably meant well …

A bit puzzled by your reference to a pet goat. Didn't know you had such a thing, old boy. Where do you keep it? You certainly are a man of mystery.

I gave Nasroodeen a little lecture on *sattvic* food, as you wisely suggested.

'Stuff and nonsense!' was his reaction. 'You cannot beat a boiled egg in the morning!'

'That's an old chestnut!' I riposted, coolly. And do you know what he served up that evening? Roasted chestnuts. I must say they were rather delicious.

We miss you!

Om shanti shanti shanti!

Krishnamurphy

PS. Hurry back.

Dear Murph,

Namaste! I am sorry to hear you are all having the runs. Try *kuzo*, mountain arrowroot.

Me? I am still standing around and sweeping a good deal. It is wonderful to be of service to the temple. Sweeping is such an amazing activity! Sweep, sweep, sweep – and the mind becomes very clear. Sweeping inside, sweeping outside. Simultaneously. This is the trick. All the time. And it's so simple. I would love to be going to the White House and teaching it to the President. He should know all about it. Also the Pope. I am saying the word over and over, 'Sweep! Sweep!' is what I am saying softly and I am sounding like some kind of an extinct bird.

I must not become too attached to the sweeping. You told me once, Krishnamurphy, that no man of our time was born without an ego, except Sunyata, that strange Danish fellow.

'I love the way you walk, it's so cute,' said a lady from San Diego to me. 'Would you come back with me and be my K9 ambulator?' I don't think she liked the way I walked away from her. Not snootily or anything but … what is a K9 ambulator? I have asked many learned pundits and numerologists here – including a Tantrika from Varanasi who is reputed to be omniscient – but none seems to know. I will sweep it out of my mind.

A Swiss tourist cocked his ear as he heard me saying the 'Sweep! Sweep!' thing and he asks me, 'Can you teach me that mantra?' I say, 'No, it is a special mantra, only for sweepers'. Is the world crazy or what? But I noticed that he recorded it nonetheless. Will he go back to

Switzerland and start muttering 'Sweep! Sweep!'? Hoping to win the sweepstake he is, I am sure of it. They will lock him up – in a cuckoo clock.

I will be back soon. Maybe sooner than you are thinking. I will, of course, have some fresh, green leaves from the holy tree for the Nothing Soup. Nothing would give me greater pleasure than to be making the soup for all of you now, especially in your condition.

> Sweepingly yours,
> Cook

PS. I am terrifically puzzled you are not knowing about my little goat. Last kid goat I am having was kidnapped and offered as sacrifice to goddess Kali. Later I am hearing that its last bleat was a prayer to the Great Mother: '*Ma!*'

Truly a reincarnation of the great poet Ramprasad, both now of blessed memory.

Beloved Cook,

It must be hot over there. I am sending you a bottle of Irish rainwater. Also a little money. By the way, I'm not surprised that the numerologists were stumped by the K9 ambulator... I think the lady meant 'canine ambulator' or dog walker.

I was thinking recently of one of your satsangs. Remember the funny girl from Iceland, with the pigtails? You started off with Om shanti shanti shanti and before the reverberations died down, little Miss Pigtails accosted you. 'I was told that you instructed someone to tell me to cover up,' she said and accused you of being anti-sex or Taliban or something. How I laughed at what you said. You may not remember. You said: 'No, not anti-sex! Trouble is you are having two legs, two eyes, two ears, two breasts. All this is reminding us of of Duality. One-legged girls need not cover up!' I laughed until I cried.

Dearest Murph,

Thank you for all your letters which awaited me on my escape from captivity. Some money fell out of your envelope – thank you ever so much – but a cow (by name of Winston) ate it.

I was kidnapped by terrorists, in suits. I don't think they told anyone about it so it might not have been in the newspapers or on your telewision screens. Anyway, people are disappearing all the time. They would want a special tea wee channel for all of it.

They gave me nothing to eat for nine whole days – which suited me fine. They threatened to chop my head off and play Western music very loud in my little cell. I say, 'Chop! Fine! Chop head. I am not living in the head anyway – do it, make a clean sweep of it.' They didn't.

They were asking me many many questions which were totally meaningless to me. I am not knowing what kind of crazy people they are – maybe canine perambulators, for all I know. Or something worse? They injected me with a truth serum but, of course, it had no effect. 'I am speaking Truth. Truth and I are one,' I say in all honesty. 'Even if you are injecting me with a lie serum, I am still speaking Truth.' They laughed at me and said there is no such a thing as a lie serum. What do they know? It was only when they laugh that I am detecting they are Americanos.

'A plane is coming to take you to Guantánamo Bay,' they say. What is this Guantánamo Bay, Murph? Is it a resort? They are torturing me and then they are chartering a plane to take me to a resort? Maybe it is a place full of half-clothed maidens splashing in the salt-flavoured sea? Little Miss Pigtails in bikini? No, Murph, they are not getting a rise out of me. No siree!

I am seeing how they are working – good cop, bad cop (I once saw a film you know. I remember the actor's name. Robert the Neero. Has he been to the ashram? He looks like he could do with some of my soup). So, anyway, they are trying this way and that way to get lots of information out of me. What information? Is God playing some of His funny tricks on me again? I must tell you, if I am getting a chance, about some of the tricks He plays. You wouldn't believe it! Once He changed me into an elephant. But that's another story. How you call it? A shagging dog story or something like that.

Anyway, while they were electrocuting my genitals – something I didn't feel at all as I counteracted their un-manly efforts with a spontaneous flow of kundalini – no anger, mind you – which blew their generator to smither-eens – suddenly I felt like eating a ripe orange and found myself walking through the wall, out into the open air and now I am safely back here in the bosom of my broth-ers in the temple who are not even knowing I was gone.

Apart from that, nothing peculiar.

Your Cook

Dearest Murphy,

Is everything OK? The omniscient Tantrika from Varanasi told me last night that I would not be returning to you. He says I am staying here. Things are falling apart – but in a good way – back at the ashram, he informs me. I do not know how he is knowing this. Is it so? I am not hearing from you, in letters. In my heart I am hearing you – and I see that you are closing the ashram down.

I must stay here to sweep every day, he says. It is important. It is not that my heart is torn between this place and yours. No. I like it here. I like it there. I like it everywhere. But this strange man – whisper it to no one, he is 205 years of age – he is telling me this: 'Your sweeping is having a subtle effect on the world – a powerful effect! Sweep,' he says, 'and forget everything else.'

I am deciding he is perfectly right. Some are born to sweep, others have sweeping thrust upon them. If you are ever coming here and visiting the Good Tree, ask for me.

Your Cook

Dear Cook,

Forgive long silence. Distressed to hear about your encounter with the Americans.

I'm afraid when you get back – if you ever do – I'll no longer be here. It's time to chuck it all in. It's getting too big. Unable to curtail it any longer. Must close down whole operation. Immediately.

The gospel was always Spiritual Anarchy – or meant to be so: a bit of this and a bit of that. It's a hard act, to build sandcastles only to destroy them. But our mission was always to subvert – not to convert.

It was all about breaking down the fortresses of illusion, bringing the mighty walls of ego crashing down, with carefree song and laughter, with fearless dialogue and even with the odd deflating, cutting jibe. And your Soup, of course, in which you poured the silence of your soul.

All was said and done in good faith, but every word, every action was open to misinterpretation. Also, the media were snooping around again. Nasroodeen gave them a terrific welcome – with a horsewhip. But I know that you do not like to hear such stories.

Anyway, how can I continue if I have to employ 20 or more security guards, more accountants and secretaries, revise insurance schemes, order light bulbs, publish books? How many Sufi poets does it take to change a light bulb? None, they are enlightened already!

I'm shutting down the shop, my Friend, so that the notion of Spiritual Anarchy can survive in some other form, or none. Somewhere else, without an institution, without walls. Keeping the show running doesn't make much sense to me anymore. Only one in ten thousand seekers is sincere. A sculptress once explained the word 'sincere' to me. I don't know if she was having me on or not. It means 'sine cera', she said, 'without wax'. If a second-rate sculptor chipped the piece he was working on, he would fill it in with wax and the flaw would be invisible. Not so the sincere artist, says she – no wax in his tool bag.

I'm rambling. It's because this is my last letter to you. And I'm a bit sad, in a way. Yes, the Sadguru is now a sad guru ...

I am enclosing a copy of our little booklet, a transcript of the memorable seminar, under your inspired direction, *Happiness is a Crow*. Sales have gone through the roof!

What will you do? What you have always done, I suppose. And I? What will I do? What will the wind do? Blow off in another direction. Become a crosswind, a breeze, a storm or, as the haiku says, hide a while among the bamboos when the storm dies down. I know not for sure.

Is the wind really free or is there an incredible harmony behind its unpredictable wantonness?

I know the answer to all that already. So do you. But I will go with the wind nonetheless. If the wind takes me.

I may have been the teacher, but who was my Teacher? I will tell you now. It was you. None other than you. All along. I could have done nothing without you. Your cooking, your sweeping, your example. Your silence. Your innocence. It was your scent really. It heralded your presence. It lingered long after you. It lingers still.

Your orangey zest captured us all, enveloped us, wafting us towards the infinite possibilities of wakefulness.

How is it you came here in the first place? What was it that guided you? Surely it was our needs that guided you, not your own – since you have none.

So, the omniscient Tantrika from Varanasi was perfectly right. Here – thousands of miles from you – I can feel the gentle rhythm of your sweeping. I see it! I hear it! It is as if you are rocking a cradle!

Farewell, Master!

Watch out for K9 ambulators...

> Love and blessings from your devoted
> Krishnamurphy and from the people and
> the crows of Ireland

Happiness Is a Crow

A seminar conducted by Cook in the Year of Nothing

Hark how the crow in the grey morning crows! Maybe this was the language of call used among the first brothers.

Miodrag Pavlovi

a crow calls

and I, too,

am alone

Santõka

Q: At your suggestion, we have all adopted a crow. What should we give him to eat?

A: Give him worms and he will become wriggly.

You can give him anything that doesn't wriggle or squirm.

Seeds.

He is not too stuffy.

Q: Fussy?

A: Yes, it is a bit fussy in here.

Open a window, please.

A banana skin is fine.

Do not overfeed him or he might womit.

Q: Vomit? What about a gin and tonic now and again?

A: No.
A little champagne on his birthday.
Nothing Soup would be better still.

Q: How do I make Nothing Soup?

A: There's nothing to it.

Q: Does a crow have a penis?

A: I am thinking this is a matter for himself.

Q: Should I wash my crow?

A: No, he is washing himself.
You wash him and his colour is coming off.

Q: Ramana Maharshi had a shrine built to a crow. Is this correct?

A: So I am hearing.
Possibly an enlightened crow.

Q: What is the crow mantra?

A: Crow mantra I am learning long time ago from Sister Assumpta is in Irish:

> *Is mór an náire*
> *Do Mháire Ní Dhálaigh*
> *Bheith chun deiridh bheith chun deiridh...*

Excuse pronunciation.

The name Mháire Ní Dhálaigh is anglicised as Mary Daly.

The mantra was intoned when a crow was flying at back of flock.

This is bringing crow up to front again.

It is the mantra of our crow movement which is spreading as the crow flies.

Q: Why is it poets have written odes to nightingales and not to crows?

A: You are thinking only of the posh poets.

There are, in fact, more poems about crows than about nightingales – but you must know where to look.

Q: How can a crow make me happy or sane?

A: The mad Japanese monk – good poet, not posh poet
– Ikkyu, he is going completely sane when he is
hearing the crow in his boat on Lake Biwa.

Caaaaaaaaw!

He becomes as sane as a button.

Q: What name would you suggest for my crow?

A: Perhaps something beginning with C if a crow
begins with C in your language:

Cedric, Catherine the Great, Catullus,
Cervantes, Cernunnus, Cleopatra, Cromwell,
Conan, Chaityana, Chang, Colm ... but Colm
means a dove which might be leading to crisis of
identity.

Q: How far can a crow fly 'as the crow flies'?

A: As far as he wants.

Q: If my crow leaves me, will he come back?

A: This is a matter concerning his karma and yours
and how they are linked as far back as Cro-Magnon
man.

Q: Where should I bring my crow on a holiday?

A: Croatia.

Q: Can a crow be as faithful as a dog?

A: Absolutely!
And he not be barking at postman.

Q: Do crows like music?

A: They have a fondness for operatic arias.

Q: Will I become closer to my crow if I wear a crow's feather in my hair?

A: No. In fact this could be quite dangerous.

Q: If my crow dies, can I eat it?

A: Only with a pinch of salt.
Actually, 'to eat crow' is a metaphor and should not be taken literally.

Q: Is it true that an Anglo-Irish gentleman, on seeing the ragged condition of the crows' nests on his estate, had them all dismantled and reconstructed again?

A: Yes.
This happened in Killucan.
A long time ago.

Crows were very upset.

And they haven't forgotten it.

It is an example of the 'improving' tendency in certain kind of men which is often doing more harm than good.

You wouldn't believe some of the improving tendencies in my first teacher, Sister Assumpta. I seem to be recalling that she was from Killucan so there must be something in the water there.

Q: Can I sleep with my crow?

A: If by sleep you are meaning sleep, then I don't see why not.

Q: If I talk to my crow, how much will he understand?

A: It is depending on topic of conversation.

Lives of the Saints, such as Mirabai, St. Francis etc., this is very good fare.

But you cannot interest him in politics.

He can see through all that. The crow is also interested in astronomy and you should talk to him about the constellation Corvus which, as you know, lies somewhere between Virgo and Hydra. Not quite sure exactly. Long time since I was there.

Q: Let's say I'm having some people over for dinner or drinkies on the patio – and they don't know about the crow. Should I hide the crow?

A: When your relationship with the crow is maturing, the last thing you are wishing to do is hiding him away from friends and relations. You might as well go and hide yourself.

If the mother-in-law isn't liking it, you are dropping the mother-in-law, not the crow.

Show them all your photo albums with you and your crow.

Holidays in Croatia and so on.

Q: What if my crow gets sick?

A: Check his temperature?

If he is really miserable, call doctor.

Not vet.

Vet is putting him down.

Vet not like crow movement at all.

Less poodles.

Less money for vet.

Crow seldom sick.

Q: Should I encourage my crow to attend religious services?

A: If you wish.

The crow has an immortal soul like anybody else and religious services are useful, sometimes.

But maybe your pastor, or rabbi or whatever, might

not approve.

Let your crow crow!

This is the best religious service of all.

Q: Should I teach my crow tricks?

A: Crow not monkey, Crow just crow.

It is his crowness that you are bringing into your life, his thereness, his being.

The flame as dark as the raven, as Yannai says. Crow.

Just as he is.

Perfect.

Why you have him standing on his little head?

Q: Is it OK to watch TV together?

A: Weather reports fine.

No News.

No News good news.

Q: Will my crow lay eggs?

A: Possibly, if he is a she.

Q: As a crow owner, should I object to such phrases as 'I have a crow to pick with you?'

A: Yes.

But do not think of yourself as a crow owner. You are not owning him.

Nor is he owning you.

As your relationship develops, this is becoming clear.

Q: My crow is depressed. Any ideas?

A: Crow not normally suffering from depression. You may be cause.

Are you really appreciating crow?

Or is this just new fad?

Care for crow, grow with crow – or let him go.

Q: I have been trying to give my crow a mixed diet – seeds, berries, snails and so on. I believe crows are fond of insects. Where can I purchase good insects on line?

A: No need for purchasing insects.

Let crow out.

He will find them.

Crow knows best.

Q: I am Jewish. I wonder should I have my crow circumcised?

A: Do not even think about it.

Q: Can I teach my crow a few phrases?

A: In Welsh, yes.

And Sanskrit.

Old Irish is also acceptable.

These will suit crow very well.

Other languages are to be avoided.

Do not teach him Australian English or he will have a complete personality change and before you know it he is saying,

'Get me a beer, you bastard!'

Q: I sometimes dream about my crow. Does he dream about me?

A: Yes.

Q: I sometimes get the feeling that my crow is laughing at me.

A: Maybe he is.

Q: There aren't really any famous crows in history, are there?

A: Whose history?

Ours? What about theirs?

Q: This crow business ... you've started something
really big. I mean, it's a real craze! I was surprised
to see a crow on the cover of *Time* magazine
recently.

A: So was the crow.

Q: There are many pro-crow and anti-crow groups
springing up in society and people are becoming
quite vociferous about the whole matter.

A: Don't blame the crow. Blame society.

Q: I want to do new things with my crow.

A: Just let crow be crow.

Not riding a bicycle or dancing a jig.

The whole meaning of the crow movement is simply
to witness the crowicity of the crow, from hour
to hour, to take the mind away from all worries and
mundane affairs, to sink into crow, to be crow.

Become humble and simple like crow.

Love the beak, the plumage, the hunger of the crow,
the poise, the stillness, the legs, the eye, the nervous
energy, the raucousness, the silence, the alertness,
the lack of gaudiness and show, the wisdom of the
crow.

Q: My crow died. What happens when a crow dies? Is
    there a heaven? I have had him stuffed but I would
    love to know what has happened to his spirit.

A: Stuffed crow is abomination.

    Heaven?

    Heaven is not an exclusive club for men and
    peacocks.

    Why should a crow not go to heaven?

    If you believe in heaven …

Q: My crow smiled at me. Was I imagining it?

A: No. And even if you were, what harm?

Q: I don't have a crow or any intention of having one.
    I mean, the whole thing is crazy. Look at all the
    problems in the world, it's unbelievable and this
    crow-craze has taken over. Are we all totally mad or
    what?

A: It's perfectly obvious you are not having a crow.

    Maybe crow doesn't want you either.

    You have heard Krishnamurphy's Gaelic curse:

    'Mallacht na bpréachán ort'.

Q: Which is to say?

A: The curse of the crows on you!

Q: Meaning?

A: May you give up what you are doing before you enjoy the fruits of your labour.

Q: I see …What is a kunguru?

A: It is a house crow, in Kenya.

Q: My crow was into *mouna* there for a few weeks. Complete silence. You wouldn't believe it. Not a twitch out of him, not a word. And then, suddenly, out of the blue – 'Caw!' It floored me. It was the most beautiful thing I ever heard in my life.

A: I believe you.

It is the blessing of Ikkyu, rediscovered in our time.

A ripple from Lake Biwa.

Q: Someone stole my crow. What should I do? Broke in and stole my crow he did. No use reporting it or offering a reward. Had no special features. Wasn't an albino or nothin'. A perfectly ordinary crow. And someone stole it.

A: Get another one.

Q: How many crows have you known?

A: None.

You never get to know a crow.

That's the great thing about it.

The mystery.

The challenge.

It's the whole point of it really.

He'll probably get to know more about you than you are ever knowing about him.

Q: Had a staring match with my crow. He won.

A: Doesn't surprise me.

Q: Can you teach yoga to a crow?

A: Crow is already doing upa yoga.

Q: What is upa yoga?

A: Attentiveness.

You are having a banana?

Crow is attentive.

He is wanting to see what's left ... he is wanting to take the crumbs from your table.

He is not watching the news on television.

He is waiting for leftovers.

This is attentiveness.

Upa yoga!

Jains says this is best yoga.

Not standing on head.

Q: My crow is a thief.

A: So, what is he stealing?

Your credit card?

He's just moving things around a bit.

No harm.

Live with it.
Learn from it.

A: OK, my question is a bit spooky... Where do I begin? The crow's name is Canute. OK? He can come into a room without my knowing it. After a while I feel his presence. Which one of us is psychic?

A: Crow, probably.

Silent type, eh?

He's probably a thinker, you know?

Maybe he's trying to figure out what's going on in your head – studying you from behind, wondering if you're some kind of an illusion or something.

It is best when you are not trying deliberately to get into their minds – or they in yours.

I am recommending some aromatherpay oils for thinking crows.

Wild indigo is one such treatment.

It might be doing the both of you some good.

A six week course and you will not be caring one way or the other; you will both be fine and relaxed, unsuspicious of one another's motifs.

Q: My mother-in-law came to dinner and was very surprised that our crow was served first. She didn't know much about the crow movement and was offended. I tried to explain and it became a bit of a shouting match and the crow became upset.

A: Yes, these things are happening for a reason.

It is all this hierarchy and labelling in life – boss, mother-in-law, ayatollah, bishop.

When a crow is introduced to this equation, we begin to look at our human institutions again and ask ourselves do we really need all this baggage.

The crow is introducing a re-balancing act into our lives.

Look at a crow and you will ask yourself have I lost something strange, something deep, something simple, something fundamental, something mysterious in my life and, in fact, we are putting a huge burden on the crow to help us transmogrify everything and allow us to reconnect with who we are.

And with our essential freedom.

The crow is capable of taking on mankind's loss of

direction as his responsibility.

In that glance from the crow, all wars can end. He unravels us.

He simplifies us.

He exposes us.

Humbles us.

He helps us to love him.

And ourselves. To be tolerant and forgiving.
Aware.

For he is bold and asserive – and sly if needs be – and is the darker side of us that is longing for the light.

And he can teach us *manolaya*, a temporary stilling of the mind.

Hundreds are experiencing it.

Some are even gifted by the crow with *manonasa*, permanent stilling of the mind.

Is wonderful, no?

And crow loves his mate.

And that is why we will free him, to find his mate – once he has taught us a thing or two – so that he may snuggle down in his nest, one with his mate and, eventually, forget us.

Forever.